John CHEEVER

a reference guide

A
Reference
Guide
to
Literature

Ronald Gottesman
Editor

John CHEEVER

a reference guide

FRANCIS J. BOSHA

G.K.HALL &CO.

70 LINCOLN STREET, BOSTON, MASS.

Library of Congress Cataloging in Publication Data
Main entry under title:

John Cheever: a reference guide.

  Bibliography: p. 1.
  Includes index.
  1. Cheever, John—Bibliography. I. Bosha,
Francis J.
Z8165.2.J63   [PS3505.H6428] 016.813'52 80-27510
ISBN 0-8161-8447-X

This publication is printed on permanent/durable acid-free paper
MANUFACTURED IN THE UNITED STATES OF AMERICA

Contents

THE AUTHOR: Francis J. Bosha completed his undergraduate work in English at the University of Scranton, received an M.A. from the Pennsylvania State University, and a Ph.D. in Twentieth Century American Literature from Marquette University. He has taught at Marquette University as an assistant professor, and is presently an associate professor of American literature at Aoyama Gakuin University in Tokyo.

His publications include: The Textual History and Definitive Textual Apparatus for "Soldiers' Pay": A Bibliographic Study of William Faulkner's First Novel and a number of articles on William Faulkner, Ezra Pound, and Mark Twain. He has also contributed entries to the Dictionary of American Biography and American Writers Before 1800, and serves as an associate bibliographer of the MLA International Bibliography.

Preface

The compilation in this reference guide of articles, reviews, and interviews with Cheever published in the United States is intended to be comprehensive, and traces his critical reception from 1943 through 1979. It should be noted, however, that although reviews of Cheever's work have appeared in many American newspapers, those covered in this guide are representative. In addition to the New York Times, major papers such as the Washington Post, the Chicago Tribune, the St. Louis Post-Dispatch and the Los Angeles Times, along with occasional pieces from other dailies, have been selected to indicate the range of Cheever's reception across the country.

This guide also provides annotations of a representative number of foreign reviews of Cheever's work. In many cases the reviews were annotated from photocopies sent by the various publishers, and these often lacked page numbers. They are otherwise complete and have been annotated here to provide an indication of Cheever's international reception, and do not purport to be exhaustive.

Thus, this reference guide consists of three sections: a chronologically arranged primary bibliography of Cheever's work published in the United States and abroad; annotated citations, also chronologically arranged, of critical, biographical, and bibliographical studies of Cheever, including interviews he has given; and an index to the authors of the secondary pieces, the titles of works mentioned in these articles, and significant recurrent terms and names.

I would like to thank the following people who helped me prepare this book:

First, John Cheever, who kindly informed me about the publication of his work abroad; Mike Gerrard, of Deborah Rogers Ltd., Mr. Cheever's British literary agent who helped me gain access to a number of foreign reviews; and the various publishers of Cheever's work abroad, who sent me copies of the reviews from their files.

I appreciate also the invaluable cooperation of Marquette University Library's interlibrary loan staff, Patricia Bohack and Ellen Murphy, and Harry J. Onufrock of the reference department. I am also grateful to the following individuals who translated material for this project: Eileen Frenn (Spanish), Joseph Frenn (French), Alexander Greenberg (Russian), Anna Øverland (Norwegian), David Mel Paul (Swedish), Giulio Risi-Valdettaro (Italian), and Richard B. Vowles (Danish).

For providing me with articles and information, thanks also to Bryan F. Griffin, Helen Mofsen, Patricia Papangelis, Rhoda Sirlin, Robert M. Slabey, and John Updike.

Introduction

From publishing his first short story in the New Republic at the age of eighteen to receiving the Pulitzer Prize for The Stories of John Cheever in 1979, nearly fifty years later, John Cheever's literary career has been characterized by early and steady publishing success, if not by comparable steady serious critical recognition.

This inconsistent critical response may be attributable in part to the fact that Cheever has published half of his more than 200 pieces of short fiction in the New Yorker magazine, with the result that, to many reviewers, a Cheever story came to connote at once the wit, irony and bored sophistication associated with that magazine. All too often this simplification has led some critics to minimize Cheever's achievement as our mid-century "chronicler of the suburbs." And yet, while sharing many of the mannerisms and even much of the subject matter of his fellow New Yorker writers, Cheever has, as Melvin Maddocks (1957.21) noted, "not been satisfied with the underdone ironies, [and] the tightly controlled grimaces" that recur in this type of fiction. It is Cheever's compassion for his characters, combined with sophistication and lyrical style that distinguishes his work. In fact, the tradition within which Cheever writes is closer to that of Nathaniel Hawthorne than to the mannered tales of John O'Hara and J. P. Marquand. The moral tone that resonates through so much of Cheever's fiction may well find its source in his New England heritage rather than his subsequent life in Manhattan and its exurbs.

John Cheever was born in Quincy, Massachusetts on May 27, 1912, and is descended from a New England family of ship's captains and clergymen who were contemporaries of Cotton Mather. Cheever grew up in a Victorian house, the son of a successful shoe factory owner, and recalls that his English maternal grandmother read him the complete works of Dickens. Early in his life he was attracted to the idea of writing for a living, and announced his plan to his parents at the age of eleven. After careful consideration they told their son: "It's all right with us if you want to be a writer, so long as you are not seeking fame or wealth." When Cheever was fifteen his father left the family and, after selling his business and investing the profit, lost everything in the 1929 crash. Cheever's mother' then supported her two sons by opening a small seaside gift shop.

Introduction

It was also in 1929 that Cheever's literary career began when he was expelled from Thayer Academy for smoking. He chronicled the event in the story "Expelled" and sent it off to Malcolm Cowley, who accepted it for publication in the October 1, 1930 issue of the New Republic. With that first, auspicious publication, "Jon" Cheever, as he would spell his first name for the next two years, began writing in earnest.

After making a walking tour of Europe in 1931 with his older brother, Frederick, Cheever decided to live in New York City and pursue his career. Hazel Hawthorne, a Boston acquaintance and wife of the biographer of P. T. Barnum, found Cheever a job writing summaries of novels for M.G.M. Meanwhile, Malcolm Cowley became something of a surrogate father as well as literary mentor for Cheever. Besides publishing some of Cheever's early stories, Cowley was responsible for introducing Cheever's work to Katherine White of the New Yorker. The appearance of "Brooklyn Rooming House" in the May 25, 1935 issue of the New Yorker was the start of regular sales for the twenty-two-year-old writer, and a publishing relationship that would continue to the present. Cowley also encouraged Cheever to attend Elizabeth Ames' Yaddo Writers' Colony, where he would stay for a month and then return sporadically.

In New York, Cheever met a number of older writers including Sherwood Anderson, John Dos Passos (whom Cheever thought "dull but pleasant"), Edmund Wilson ("we both detested one another"), Dorothy Parker, Archibald MacLeish, and his close friend, E. E. Cummings. Cheever explained in an interview that "Cummings was very exciting and very helpful. I was in the army for four years, in an infantry company, and got a letter from him which included a ten-dollar bill, an autumn leaf, and the line, 'I too have slept with someone else's boot in the corner of my smile'" (1977.40).

By 1943 Cheever had published over forty stories and collected thirty of them for his first book, The Way Some People Live. For a first book of stories, this collection was reasonably well received and, though some reviewers detected a sameness in the various vignettes, others at least found the style "compelling" and the twists of irony noteworthy.

Ten years later, the publication of The Enormous Radio and Other Stories, a collection that was more successful, marked Cheever's progress out of his years of apprenticeship. Many of these fourteen stories revealed that, despite the persistent simplification of some critics, Cheever was more than an observer of middle-class suburban manners. Some of these pieces were set in New York City, while others used the seaside, a farm, and even a ski resort for locales. In addition, his protagonists now included an elevator operator among the middle-class apartment dwellers and affluent suburbanites. His range was now broader than his first book indicated, and his moral vision was increasingly evident in such pieces as the title story, with its Hawthornian overtones of a young couple's loss of innocence. In his 1953 review of this collection, William Peden sounded a theme that would persist for the next twenty-five years: "Cheever is one of our most undervalued American short story writers" (1953.15).

During the 1950s Cheever began to garner a number of awards and encomiums, including a Guggenheim Fellowship in 1951, the Benjamin Franklin Magazine Award for the best story of 1954, and two O. Henry story awards. Although his reputation was growing, it was still as a short story writer; in 1957, however, Cheever published his first novel, The Wapshot Chronicle, which won the National Book Award the following year.

In The Wapshot Chronicle Cheever drew on his memories of his family; parallels are evident between a number of the events and characters in the work and those of his own life, despite Cheever's oft-stated denial that his fiction is not "crypto-autobiography." Critics complained that Cheever had loosely tied a number of related stories together and had created an episodic work that reflected both the strengths and weaknesses of the short story. Such criticism now seems beside the point; Cheever's achievement here was not formal but lay instead in the discovery of his most deeply felt subject matter and most characteristic theme: the celebration of life in St. Botolphs, an idealized New England village belonging more to the last century than to the present. Some commentators have since drawn analogies between this mythic village and Faulkner's town of Jefferson. Moreover, the nostalgia present in the novel runs through much of Cheever's work. As he explained to an interviewer: "Nostalgia is the longing for the world we all know, or seem to know, the world we all love, and the people in it we love" (1977.40).

The following year Cheever published his third book of short stories, The Housebreaker of Shady Hill, which contains some of his best known work. In fact, in addition to being widely anthologized, three of these stories, "The Sorrows of Gin," "O Youth and Beauty," and "The Five Forty-Eight" were adapted into teleplays and broadcast on the Public Broadcasting System in the Fall of 1979. From the standpoint of formal development in Cheever's fiction, most of these stories relied on an omniscient and often intrusive narrator, a technique Cheever would pursue in a number of stories in his next collection and in his second novel. In his depiction of the often adolescent values and broken dreams of his suburbanites, however, one is still able to recognize Cheever's distinctive moral vision. He revealed himself, that is, as a "compassionate ironist" who avoided sentimentality, leading Commonweal to conclude that Cheever had become the "Dante of Suburbia" (1958.7).

The title of his next book, Some People, Places, and Things That Will Not Appear in My Next Novel (1961) was derived from a conceit, as Cheever explained in his preface, concerning his desire to "exorcise" certain characters and situations from his writing by using them here for the last time. He reasoned that "in order to become readable again, . . . fiction can no longer operate as a sixth-rate boarding house." He elaborated on this idea in his closing story, "A Miscellany of Characters That Will Not Appear," and decreed that he was eliminating "all parts for Marlon Brando. . . . All scornful descriptions of American landscapes . . . explicit descriptions of sexual commerce. . . . All lushes. . . . [and] homosexuals," among others. However, a reading of Cheever's subsequent three novels will challenge the view that this is a serious "declaration of intent" (1964.51).

A few of the other pieces in this collection introduced a new element in Cheever's fiction: the experience of Americans in Italy. This has led some critics to draw parallels between Cheever, Henry James, and Nathaniel Hawthorne. In later stories, and even in his second novel, Cheever would develop this theme of innocents abroad. Certain of these pieces, and others in the collection, also reveal a darker side of the writer that had theretofore not been so apparent, and so some reviewers began to comment on Cheever's "gothic" and even "Kafkaesque" dimensions.

Nineteen sixty-four brought the publication of two books: a sequel to The Wapshot Chronicle, The Wapshot Scandal, and another book of stories, The Brigadier and the Golf Widow. Many reviewers found The Wapshot Scandal disappointing and noted that it was even more carelessly constructed than its predecessor. Elizabeth Hardwick added that it was deformed by "bits of Our Townism" (1964.31). By contrasting the modern technocracy and its attendant ills to the peaceful world of St. Botolphs, Cheever subordinated characterization to theme. The Wapshot Scandal, it was claimed, emerges as an episodic work that mixed social criticism with elements of broad comedy and nostalgia, with the result that many who had enjoyed The Wapshot Chronicle were now baffled.

In The Brigadier and the Golf Widow, Cheever introduced a mythopoeic and at times nightmarish element in such stories as "The Swimmer" and "Metamorphoses," which led one reviewer to call him a "haunted entertainer" (1964.45). Throughout this collection Cheever revealed the insecurities of his seemingly secure characters, and traced the fear that resides beneath the veneer of suburban smugness. He also returned to his expatriate theme in "Clementina," depicting the tragic conflict of being from two different cultures yet belonging in neither. The nightmarish and surrealistic overshadow the nostalgic throughout. In 1965 The Wapshot Scandal won the Howells Medal, and in 1968 "The Swimmer" was made into a movie with Burt Lancaster in the starring role.

Bullet Park (1969), Cheever's third novel, was an extreme and even bizarre departure from the Wapshot sagas. The chief reaction of the reviewers was confusion. Many were disturbed by the attempted crucifixion at the end, which Guy Davenport described as "pure hokum"

(1969.16). Though Bullet Park shares with Cheever's two earlier
novels a weak structure, this novel's grotesque religious symbolism
and use of madness led some to find the novel a "brilliant" exposé
and even a "masterpiece" (1969.28), though most reviewers agreed
with Roderick Nordell's conclusion that it "does not pay to puzzle
at" the allegorical implications (1969.34). Two years after this
storm of critical reaction passed, John Gardner (1971.2) suggested
that the reason behind the frequently hostile response to Bullet Park
was annoyance at Cheever's intimation that good and evil are merely
the effects of chance. Gardner instead found the novel "magnificent"
and superior to the Wapshot novels. Bullet Park was a moderate publishing success in this country, but sold more copies in the Soviet
Union when released in translation in 1970.[1]

In The World of Apples (1973), Cheever's next collection of
stories, he returned to his familiar concerns where, as one reviewer
found, "memory is the chief force, quaintness and innocence the basic
values; violence is subdued in nostalgia" (1973.6). Still, many felt
that Cheever was simply a whimsical writer and had worked this vein
too thoroughly. Robert Phillips noted that this book "is as important to the Cheever canon as a carbon copy is to its bright original"
(1973.31). Yet there were those who were taking Cheever more seriously, and in 1973 he became the subject of a doctoral dissertation
on the "dual vision of his art" (1973.36), and the following year
two more dissertations were written on Cheever. Meanwhile, he was
elected to membership in the American Academy of Arts and Letters in
1973, spent 1974 as a writer-in-residence at the University of Iowa,
and the next year served in that capacity at Boston University.

Despite these professional honors, Cheever's personal life had
begun to unravel. After two heart attacks and decades of heavy
drinking, Cheever felt that his life and career were over. Yet,
encouraged by his family and friends, he admitted himself into a
detoxification center in 1975 and has since been recovering from
alcoholism. He discusses the problem openly, and recently pointed
out that when drinking heavily, "I never went near the typewriter. . . .

----

1. John Cheever has had the good fortune of publishing widely
outside the United States since 1953, when The Enormous Radio and
Other Stories was published in London. The publication of Cheever's
work in translation began in 1958, with the Italian and German editions of The Wapshot Chronicle. Since that time, all of Cheever's
fiction, except The World of Apples, has been translated into at
least fifteen languages. Of all these non-English speaking nations,
the Soviet Union has provided Cheever with his largest audience. In
fact, the run of Bullet Park exceeded 100,000 copies, and became a
better seller in the USSR than in the USA. Cheever ranks just
below Updike as the favorite contemporary American writer in Russia,
and is looked upon as a social realist who condemns bourgeois and
capitalistic values.

Introduction

I think you can detect alcohol in writing the way you can detect
Latin. Only one is an advantage, and the other is not" (1977.40).

By 1976 Cheever was the "representative" American novelist whom
Newsweek asked to contribute an essay for their bicentennial issue.
In that piece Cheever restated certain of his earlier themes, noting
that this country still has "a newness, . . . a freshness," and that
America is "haunted by a dream of excellence."

Although some reviewers were surprised by what appeared to be a
departure in Falconer (1977), his fourth novel, a few critics saw
that this novel of Ezekiel Farragut's incarceration and eventual
escape from Falconer prison differed only superficially from
Cheever's earlier work. The principal factor here was that the
prison setting was no different, spiritually, from the psychic
enclosures Cheever's characters endured in Shady Hill or Bullet
Park. Some, like Richard Locke, saw "symbolic Christian realism"
in Falconer (1977.52), and Janet Groth described the novel as "a
stunning meditation on all forms of confinement and liberation"
(1977.35). Robert Towers added that Falconer contained "much that
has been implicit in Cheever's fiction all along" (1977.72).

In June 1978 Cheever received academic recognition that especially
pleased him: Harvard University awarded him an honorary doctorate.
As one writer noted, Cheever "seems to find something Cheeveresque in
the ultimate university's honoring of a failed preppie" (1978.65).

Later in 1978 Cheever gathered sixty-one stories he had written
since 1945 and published The Stories of John Cheever. This book became a best-seller and was viewed as "a grand occasion in English
literature" (1978.54). Cheever himself noted that these stories "are
very much my voice. They're not what is known as New Yorker stories.
I hadn't imagined them ever being collected, so I had no self-
consciousness that they would make a sum, but they do. They represent the span of my life, and hundreds of people I've known and
imagined" (1978.65). These stories revealed Cheever to be, in Irwin
Shaw's phrase, "a judge of stern moral standards who unerringly dis-
covers the lie beneath the candid stare, . . . the despair buried in
the hilarity of the Saturday night dance" (1978.67). This collection
won the Pulitzer Prize and the National Book Critics Circle Award,
and even revived speculation made the previous year that Cheever
would be a contender for the Nobel Prize.

Today, Cheever and his wife Mary, whom he wed in 1941, live in a
200-year old house in suburban Ossining, New York, with their three
Labrador retrievers. He numbers among his friends Irwin Shaw, Saul
Bellow, and Bernard Malamud, and observes that "in my generation of
writers, there is no nastiness, it seems to me. It's something we
learned from the previous generation. Faulkner, Hemingway, Fitz-
gerald--they couldn't get along" (1977.39).

Introduction

John Updike, another close friend, and one who supported Cheever through his recovery from alcoholism, has often been compared to Cheever as a writer. They have both published more short fiction in the New Yorker than any other writer, save John O'Hara, and have frequently used suburban settings in their work. Yet there are differences, as Cheever recently explained to an interviewer: "Well, I'm 20 years older than John. . . . Updike writes far more explicitly about sex, for one thing. Explicit sexual scenes don't particularly interest me. Everybody knows what's going on. I can't think, in the whole history of literature, of an explicit sex scene that was memorable, can you?" (1979.29).

In September 1979 Cheever was awarded the Edward MacDowell Medal "for outstanding contribution to the arts," a tribute Cheever described as "exceptional for me in that the medal has only been given to those people who have been highly estimable colleagues and in a few instances, dear friends" (1979.22).

Writings by John Cheever

Writings by John Cheever

Books

The Way Some People Live. New York: Random House, 1943.

The Enormous Radio and Other Stories. New York: Funk & Wagnalls,
1953. London: Victor Gollancz, 1953. Reprint. New York:
Harper, Colophon Books, 1965. [Includes three stories from
The Way Some People Live.]

Stories. With Jean Stafford, Daniel Fuchs, and William Maxwell.
New York: Farrar, Straus and Cudahy, 1956. A Book of Stories.
London: Victor Gollancz, 1957. Reprint. New York: Farrar,
Straus & Giroux, 1966. [Special hardcover and paper editions
with an introduction by William Peden.]

The Wapshot Chronicle. New York: Harper & Brothers, 1957.
London: Victor Gollancz, 1957. Amore e la vita. Translated
by Marcella Pavolini. Milan: Loganesi, 1958. Die Lieben
Wapshots. Translated by Dr. Arno Dohn. Reinbek bei Hamburg:
Rowohlt Verlag, 1958. Reprint (paper), 1962. La Familia
Wapshot. Translated by Nieves Maturano. Barcelona:
Editorial Pomaire, 1965. Reprint. New York: Time-Life,
1965. [Edition with an introduction by the author.]
Wapshot-sagen. Translated by Knud Søgaard. Copenhagen:
Gyldendal, 1965. Les Wapshots. Translated by Genevieve
Naudin. Paris: Rene Julliard, 1965. Rodinna Kronika
Wapshotovych. Translated by Jarmilla Fastrova. Prague:
Mlada Fronta, 1967. Vart korta liv. Translated by Jane
Lundblad. Stockholm: Norstedt & Sönners Forlag, 1967.
Wapshot Chronicle. Translated by T. Rovenskaya. Moscow,
1968. Die Lieben Wapshots Und Die Schlimmen Wapshots.
Translated by Dr. Arno Dohn and Paul Baudisch, respectively
(2 vols. in 1). Darmstadt: Deutsche Buchgemeinschaft, 1962.
East Berlin: Verlag Volk und Welt, 1975. Reprint. New York:
Harper & Row, 1973.

The Housebreaker of Shady Hill and Other Stories. New York:
Harper & Brothers, 1958. London: Victor Gollancz, 1958.
Reprint. New York: Macfadden Books, 1961.

Writings by John Cheever

Books

Some People, Places and Things That Will Not Appear in My Next
Novel. New York: Harper & Brothers, 1961. London: Victor
Gollancz, 1961. Reprint. New York: Bantam, 1963. Reprint.
Freeport, N.Y.: Books for Libraries, 1970.

Dry Martini. Translated by Amalia d'Agostino Schanzer. Milan:
Loganesi, 1962. [Collection of seven stories.]

Selected Stories. Translated by Tatyana Litvinova. Moscow,
1962.

The Wapshot Scandal. New York: Harper & Row, 1964. London:
Victor Gollancz, 1964. Reprint. New York: Bantam, 1965.
El Escandolo Wapshot. Translated by Nieves Maturano.
Barcelona: Editorial Pomaire, 1965. Lo scandolo Wapshot.
Translated by Isabella Leonetti. Milan: Garzanti, 1966.
Les Wapshot II. Translated by Nicole Bloch. Paris: Rene
Julliard, 1966. Wapshot-skandalen. Translated by Knud
Søgaard. Copenhagen: Gyldendal, 1967. Die Schlimmen
Wapshots. Translated by Paul Baudisch. Reinbeck bei
Hamburg: Rowohlt Verlag, 1967. En amerkansk skandal.
Translated by Jane Lundblad. Stockholm: Norstedt & Sönners
Forlag, 1969. The Wapshot Scandal. Moscow, 1973. Reprint.
New York: Harper & Row, 1973.

The Brigadier and the Golf Widow. New York: Harper & Row, 1964.
London: Victor Gollancz, 1965. Reprint. New York: Bantam,
1965. El nada dor. Translated by Jose Luis Lopez Muñoz.
Madrid: Editorial Magisterio Español, 1968.

Homage to Shakespeare. Stevenson, Conn.: Country Squire Books,
1968. [Limited hardcover reprint of story, 150 signed copies.]

Bullet Park. New York: Alfred A. Knopf, 1969. London:
Jonathan Cape, 1969. Reprint. New York: Bantam, 1970.
Bullet Park. Translated by Knud Søgaard. Copenhagen:
Gyldendal, 1970. Chiodi e martello. Translated by Marcella
Bonsanti. Milan: Garzanti, 1970. Villastaden. Translated
by Ingeborg von Rosen. Stockholm: Norstedt & Sönners Forlag,
1970. "Bullet Park." Inostrannaya literature (Moscow),
nos. 7 & 8 (1970). Die Burger von Bullet Park. Translated
by Kurt Wagenseil. East Berlin: Verlag Volk und Welt, 1972.
Reprint. Reinbeck bei Hamburg: Rowohlt Verlag, 1975.
Reprint. New York: Ballantine, 1978. Suburbio. Translated
by Anibal Leal. Buenos Aires: Emece Editores, 1979. Bullet
Park. Translated by Guido Goluke. Amsterdam: Uitgeverij De
Arbeiderspers, 1980. Reprint. New York: Ballantine, 1980.

Writings by John Cheever

The World of Apples. New York: Alfred A. Knopf, 1973. London: Jonathan Cape, 1974. Reprint. New York: Warner, 1974.

Falconer. New York: Alfred A. Knopf, 1977. London: Jonathan Cape, 1977. Falconer. Translated by Joop van Helmond. Amsterdam: Uitgeverij De Arbeiderspers, 1977. Reprint. New York: Ballantine, 1978. Falconer. Translated by Anibal Leal. Buenos Aires: Emece Editores, 1978. Falconer faengslet. Translated by Jannick Storm. Copenhagen: Lindhardt og Ringhofs Forlag, 1978. Il Prigioniero Di Falconer. Translated by Ettore Capriolo. Milan: Garzanti, 1978. Falconer. Translated by Dieter Dorr. Munich: Droemer Knaur Verlag, 1978. Falconer. Translated by M. Michel Doury. Paris: Rene Julliard, 1978. Falconer. Translated by Trygve Greiff. Oslo: Cappelen, 1978. Falconer. Translated by Ingeborg and Per Adolf von Rosen. Stockholm: Norstedt & Sönners Forlag, 1978. Reprint: New York: Ballantine, 1980.

The Stories of John Cheever. New York: Alfred A. Knopf, 1978. London: Jonathan Cape, 1979. Reprint. New York: Ballantine, 1980.

Articles

"Happy Days." Review of The Gospel According to St. Luke's, by Philip Stevenson. New Republic 66 (6 May 1931): 336-37.

"While the Fields Burn." Review of Now in November, by Josephine Johnson. New Republic 80 (26 September 1934): 191-92.

"Way Down East." Review of Silas Crocket, by Mary Ellen Chase. New Republic 85 (11 December 1935): 146.

"The Genteel Engineer." Review of Pity the Tyrant, by Hans Otto Storm. New Republic 93 (8 December 1937): 146.

"Cape Codders." Review of Cranberry Red, by E. Garside. New Republic 98 (8 February 1939): 25.

"New Hampshire Holiday." Holiday 8 (September 1950): 56.

"Where New York Children Play." Holiday 10 (August 1951): 46.

"Author's Note." In Stories, by Jean Stafford, John Cheever, Daniel Fuchs, and William Maxwell. New York: Farrar, Straus & Cudahy, 1956.

Writings by John Cheever

Articles

"A Word from Writer Directly to Reader: John Cheever." In Fiction of the Fifties, edited by Herbert Gold, p. 21. Garden City, N.Y.: Doubleday & Company, 1959.

"Goodbye, My Brother," and "What Happened." In Understanding Fiction, 2d ed., edited by Cleanth Brooks and Robert Penn Warren, pp. 553-70, 570-72. New York: Appleton-Century-Crofts, 1959.

"Moving Out." Esquire 54 (July 1960): 67-68. Reprint. Esquire 80 (October 1973), 174-75.

Introduction to The Wapshot Chronicle, pp. xvii-xix. Time Reading Program Special Edition. New York: Time-Life, 1965.

"Sophia, Sophia, Sophia." Saturday Evening Post 240 (21 October 1967): 32-35.

"F. Scott Fitzgerald." In Atlantic Brief Lives, edited by Louis Kronenberger, pp. 275-76. Boston: Little, Brown, 1971.

"Fiction." Review of The Ewings, by John O'Hara. Esquire 77 (May 1972): 14.

"Authors' Authors." New York Times Book Review, 5 December 1976, p. 4.

"Recent Trends in Writing and Publishing." Intellect 105 (July 1976): 11-12.

"The Novelist." In "Our America: A Self-Portrait at 200," edited by Peter Goldman. Newsweek 88 (4 July 1976): 36.

"Thanks, Too, for Memories." New York Times, 22 November 1976, p. C-3.

"The Hostess of Yaddo." New York Times Book Review, 8 May 1977, p. 3.

Letter to Elizabeth Hardwick. In "An Exchange on Fiction." New York Review of Books, 3 February 1977, p. 44.

"Writers' Writers." New York Times Book Review, 4 December 1977, p. 3.

Preface to The Stories of John Cheever, pp. vii-viii. New York: Alfred A. Knopf, 1978.

"Romania." Travel and Leisure 8 (March 1978): 84.

"Why I Write Short Stories." Newsweek 92 (30 October 1978):
   24-25.

"Fiction is Our Most Intimate Means of Communication." U.S.
   News and World Report 86 (21 May 1979): 92.

"A 'True Life Novel' of a Murderer Transfigured by Death."
   Review of The Executioner's Song, by Norman Mailer. Chicago
   Tribune Book World, 7 October 1979, p. 1.

Adaptations

Tonkonogy, Gertrude. Town House (1948). [A play adapted from
   the "Town House" series of stories.]

Perry, Eleanor. The Swimmer (1966). [A screenplay adapted from
   the story, "The Swimmer."]

_____. The Swimmer. New York: Stein & Day, 1967. Reprint.
   New York: Pyramid Books, 1968. [A novel adapted from the
   screenplay.]

Gurney, A. R., Jr. Children. [A play adapted from the story,
   "Goodbye, My Brother" (1976).]

_____. O Youth and Beauty (1979). [A teleplay adapted from the
   story of the same title for the Public Broadcasting Service.]

McNally, Terrence. The Five Forty-Eight (1979). [A teleplay
   adapted from the story of the same title for the Public
   Broadcasting Service.]

Wasserstein, Wendy. The Sorrows of Gin (1979). [A teleplay
   adapted from the story of the same title for the Public
   Broadcasting Service.]

Writings about John Cheever, 1943-1979

Writings about John Cheever, 1943-1979

1 ANON. Review of The Way Some People Live. Booklist 39
    (15 May): 369.
        "Short stories that characterize individuals and groups"
    in contemporary American life.

2 ANON. "Briefly Noted." New Yorker 19 (20 March): 70.
        Review of The Way Some People Live. Finds most of these
    stories "effective and certain of them distinguished--about
    confused and suffering people."

3 BURT, STRUTHERS. "John Cheever's Sense of Drama." Saturday
    Review 26 (24 April): 9.
        Review of The Way Some People Live. Predicting that
    Cheever "will become one of the most distinguished writers,"
    the reviewer finds that at least half of these stories are
    "eminently successful." Attributes the collection's "feeling
    of a novel" to the arrangement of the stories, and praises
    "Of Love: A Testimony" as "one of the best love stories I
    have ever read." Reprinted: 1969.15.

4 DuBOIS, WILLIAM. "Tortured Souls." New York Times Book Review,
    28 March, p. 10.
        Review of The Way Some People Live. Suggests that these
    stories' "peculiar epicene detachment, and facile despair"
    may be due to their earlier appearance in the New Yorker.
    Finds that the author's "avoidance of anything resembling a
    climax" renders his stories into mere vignettes, and that his
    preoccupation with misanthropic characters "can only make for
    boredom, if you take your Cheever in large doses." Still, his
    style is compelling.

5 FELD, ROSE. "New Fiction from the Atlantic to the Pacific."
    New York Herald Tribune Weekly Book Review, 14 March, p. 12.
        Review of The Way Some People Live. Finds that only a few
    of the pieces collected here should rightly be called stories.
    Most of this writing comprises "moments or moods caught in the

11

1943

lives of his characters, pointed in quality but inconclusive in effect." The result is a book of interesting "fragments," which "leave the reader suspended in anticipation that has no artistic fulfillment." It is in a story such as "A Border Incident" that Cheever approaches the conventional story. Despite the slight material of most of these stories, however, they are all notable in the way Cheever "brings sympathy and irony to characters in the bleak moments in which he catches them."

6 KEES, WELDON. "John Cheever's Stories." New Republic 108 (19 April): 516-17.
       Review of The Way Some People Live. Although Cheever is a talented writer, much of his work suffers from the almost formulaic skill which marks them as New Yorker stories. These pieces concentrate "on the merely decorative qualities of a scene," because the New Yorker "demands a patina of triviality." Thus, some of Cheever's best stories are from his pre-New Yorker writing, and among them, "Of Love: A Testimony" "is an excellent example of what this writer is capable of doing when he is his own man, when he has room enough in which to work for something more than episodic notation and minor perceptive effects." Reprinted: 1969.15.

7 SCHORER, MARK. "Outstanding Novels." The Yale Review 32 (Summer): xii, xiv.
       Review of The Way Some People Live. Considers Cheever "among the most promising of the younger short story writers" and cites "Of Love: A Testimony" as an indication of this. This story "spreads in every way--in time, in space, in point of view, in the nature of analysis" and then tightens its focus. Reprinted: 1969.15.

8 TRILLING, DIANA. "Fiction in Brief." The Nation 156 (10 April): 533.
       Review of The Way Some People Live. Argues that to read these stories "is to end with an intense feeling of frustration," because they tend to be only "strongly worded hints rather than completely communicated statements." Finds that refusing to articulate for inarticulate characters "is an artificial and completely self-imposed limitation" that Cheever would do well to get rid of.

1948

1 GABRIEL, GILBERT W. "The Broadway Story." Theatre Arts 32 (October): 14.

Mentions the Max Gordon production of "Town House,"
adapted from Cheever's story "of the intricacies of co-
operative housing."

<u>1953</u>

1 ANON. Review of <u>The Enormous Radio and Other Stories</u>. <u>Booklist</u>
49 (15 May): 303.
Finds that in these stories Cheever's "clipped, precise
style" tends to conceal "his real sympathy" for his
characters.

2 ANON. Review of <u>The Enormous Radio and Other Stories</u>. <u>U.S.
Quarterly Book Review</u> 9 (September): 297–98.
Despite their "monotonously wry and acrid quality," these
stories effectively communicate the destructiveness of American materialistic competitiveness. Notes that it is only on
"rare occasions" that Cheever's stories have a happy ending,
and that then "the effect of it is not always imaginative."

3 ANON. Review of <u>The Enormous Radio and Other Stories</u>. <u>Virginia
Kirkus Service</u> 21 (15 February): 127.
Finds that this collection reveals Cheever's "sensitivity
to discord and a feeling for contemporary conflict." These
pieces are characterized "by gentleness rather than
bitterness."

4 ANON. "Short Stories." <u>Times Literary Supplement</u> 52
(9 October): 641.
Review of <u>The Enormous Radio and Other Stories</u>. Praises
Cheever for his originality and sensitivity, yet finds "his
virtues and defects" to be typical of those found in the <u>New
Yorker</u>.

5 BLOOMFIELD, PAUL. "New Fiction." <u>Manchester Guardian</u>,
16 October, p. 4.
Review of <u>The Enormous Radio and Other Stories</u>. Finds
that these stories "have heart as well as pace." Praises
Cheever's ability to keep control of his characters and his
care in not letting them get "lost in the mechanism of their
setting."

6 BOATWRIGHT, TALIAFERRO. "Snapshots in the East Fifties." <u>New
York Herald Tribune Book Review</u>, 24 May, p. 16.
Review of <u>The Enormous Radio and Other Stories</u>. Describes
these stories as "competently done, some are excellent," but
feels that the book is better read by "dipping in" than by
reading straight through. Finds Cheever's characterizations

of the literate urbanites more effective than those of the elevator operators and notes that Cheever only seems to know the latter, lower class "externally, that what they say and do is only a projection of what he thinks they may feel and think."

7 BREIT, HARVEY. "Big Interruption." New York Times Book Review, 10 May, p. 8.
    Interview. Cheever discusses his preference for writing short stories, noting that the novel, based on nineteenth century parish life "seems artificial." The short story is determined "by the interrupted event."

8 DuBOIS, WILLIAM. "Books of the Times." New York Times, 1 May, p. 19.
    Review of The Enormous Radio and Other Stories. Finds that Cheever epitomizes the New Yorker style, conveying that magazine's "brilliant, bitter essence," and notes that these stories "will repay the closest study." While Cheever's narrow setting for these pieces is not a liability, his "too-narrow outlook" is: his "characters are even more restricted than their stamping ground." The result is a portrait of "emotional dwarfs" that is "chillingly accurate--and very much the same." Cheever writes vividly, but the melancholy sameness of his work makes it difficult to read these stories in sequence and leads one to "wonder if the human race, as Mr. Cheever views it, is worth saving."

9 FREEDMAN, MORRIS. "New England and Hollywood." Commentary 16 (October): 389-90, 392.
    Review of The Enormous Radio and Other Stories. Considers Cheever to be "a product of the Hebraic New England conscience implacable as a Kafkaesque judge," who can be compassionate and still bare "a human problem to the bone." Yet Cheever transcends Kafka's bleakness in many of these stories and demonstrates that "salvation lies in meeting the unavoidable horror head on, and engaging it with one's best talents, not obscuring it or fleeing from it." "Goodbye, My Brother" is representative of this vision.

10 HASWELL, RICHARD E. "The Enormous Hoax: One Tale Told 14 Times." St. Louis Post-Dispatch, 26 April, p. 4.
    Review of The Enormous Radio and Other Stories. Contends that these stories are really "14 variations of the same story," yet finds it is "expertly done, with such sure taste and craftsmanship." Hopes Cheever will eventually "discover another plot and write another story."

11 HOUSTON, PENELOPE. "Short Stories." The Spectator 191
    (20 November): 609-10.
        Review of The Enormous Radio and Other Stories. Finds that
    although this collection is written in a "deliberately flat,
    controlled style," Cheever is a writer with an "authentic and
    distinctive imagination." Suggests also that Cheever "may
    owe something" to John O'Hara and possibly Irwin Shaw and
    that he tends to overuse his "talent for the macabre."

12 KELLY, JAMES. "The Have-Not-Enoughs." New York Times Book
    Review, 10 May, p. 21.
        Review of The Enormous Radio and Other Stories. Despite
    the lack of a well-made plot, these stories have "plenty of
    interior mood and essence." Finds that his ironic style has
    enabled Cheever to present the truth about the lives of the
    "middle-class have-not-enoughs." In this way Cheever is able
    to "reveal New Yorkers to themselves or explain them just as
    persuasively to the reader in Steubenville, Ohio."

13 L., M. "The New Books." San Francisco Chronicle, 24 May, p. 27.
        Review of The Enormous Radio and Other Stories. Although
    these stories concern the "hidden ugliness, death, decay, or
    simply nothing" that lies beneath life's surface, Cheever
    tempers their force by his compassion. The author's warm
    understanding, in fact, "makes these stories memorable."

14 MIZENER, ARTHUR. "In Genteel Traditions." The New Republic 128
    (25 May): 19-20.
        Review of The Enormous Radio and Other Stories. Although
    Cheever "is not a writer of any great talent," his stories are
    "skillfully worked out and loaded with carefully observed man-
    ners." The problem with his stories is that they are merely
    clever and well made, but "their feeling is crude." Cheever
    emerges, through his fiction, as "a man who has ideas about
    experience but has never known these ideas in experience."
    Reprinted: 1969.15.

15 PEDEN, WILLIAM. "Esthetics of the Story." Saturday Review 36
    (11 April): 43-44.
        Review of The Enormous Radio and Other Stories. Compared
    to the stories of J. D. Salinger, Cheever's are "less spec-
    tacular," although unlike Salinger's, "they improve with re-
    reading." Praises Cheever for his ability to portray "the
    loneliness and sickness of a segment of contemporary society",
    and to make the usual into the significant. Finds that
    "Cheever is one of the most undervalued American short story
    writers."

1953

16 PICKREL, PAUL. "Outstanding Novels." The Yale Review 42
       (Summer): x, xii.
          Review of The Enormous Radio and Other Stories. Commends
       Cheever's "highly finished" writing, noting that the emotions
       are "carefully weighed and cunningly deplored." Comments also
       on Cheever's "wistful humanism," his sentimental faith in
       humanity in spite of the inanimate oppressiveness of his char-
       acters' urban setting.

1955

1 ANON. "Magazine Awards Made." New York Times, 29 May, p. 3.
          Reports that Cheever's "Five-Forty-Eight" has won the
       University of Illinois' Benjamin Franklin Magazine Award for
       the best short story of 1954.

1956

1 ANON. Review of Stories. Booklist 53 (1 January): 225.
          Finds all these stories similar in their "attention to
       craftsmanship and style."

2 ANON. Review of Stories. Virginia Kirkus Service 24
       (1 October): 764.
          Considers this collection "a happy collaboration of talent
       for fastidious tastes" and praises Cheever's rueful examina-
       tion of his characters' lives in "The Country Husband."

3 ANON. "News from the Defeated." Time 68 (3 December): 106-7.
          Review of Stories. Considers Jean Stafford to be "the
       biggest name and most accomplished craftsman in the group."
       Does not refer specifically to Cheever but finds that the
       entire collection is marked by "competence and shrewd
       observation."

4 ANON. "Two Arts Groups Make 24 Awards." New York Times, 24 May,
       p. 25.
          Reports that the American Academy and the National Insti-
       tute of Arts and Letters have awarded Cheever a $1,000 insti-
       tute grant.

5 BURNETTE, FRANCES. Review of Stories. Library Journal 81
       (1 December): 2846-47.
          Praises Cheever for his "absorbing narrative quality" and
       finds that his stories bear the New Yorker "stamp," which is
       "not a style, but a polish."

6 ENGLE, PAUL. "Superb, Brief Tales by Four American Writers."
   Chicago Sunday Tribune, 23 December, p. 5.
        Review of Stories. Praises Cheever for his "accurate ear
   for language and sharp knowledge" of his suburban characters.
   Places the theme of "The Country Husband," with its "true
   account" of one man's struggle to find meaning in his life,
   among the dominant themes of modern literature.

7 HOGAN, WILLIAM. "Prize Stories That Have Won No Prizes." San
   Francisco Chronicle, 6 December, p. 25.
        Review of Stories. Terms this collection "a performance in
   concert by four craftsmen" of the New Yorker, and finds Jean
   Stafford to be "the artist of the company represented here."
   Cheever's work is simply viewed as "entertaining."

8 MARTINEZ, RAMONA MAHER. "Book Reviews." New Mexico Quarterly
   26 (Winter 1956-57): 406-7.
        Review of Stories. Describes Cheever as a writer of "deft
   psychoanalytic stories which sunder the suburbanites where
   they wake or sleep." Praises "The Day the Pig Fell into the
   Well" for its superb control and compression.

9 NORDELL, ROD. "With 'A Kind of Hollow Good Cheer.'" Christian
   Science Monitor, 6 December, p. 11.
        Review of Stories. Finds that the collection provides "an
   uncomfortably plausible reflection of society" and that while
   the writing throughout is "tidy," the reader expects more from
   these writers of "obvious talent."

10 PEDEN, WILLIAM. "Four Cameos." Saturday Review 39 (8 December):
   15-16, 52.
        Review of Stories. Finds "that there is no finer present-
   day American writer of short fiction than John Cheever." Sum-
   marizes his four stories and notes that "The Day the Pig Fell
   into the Well" has "a variety of character and incident more
   customarily associated with the novel than with the short
   story."

11 SULLIVAN, RICHARD. "A Talented Quartet." New York Times Book
   Review, 23 December, p. 10.
        Review of Stories. Speaks generally of the collection's
   "beautifully controlled, expert, worthy and honorable pieces
   of prose" and finds that the fifteen stories are unified by a
   "worrisome concern with human behavior."

1957

1 ALLEN, WALTER. "New Novels." New Statesman 54 (12 October):
      469.
         Review of The Wapshot Chronicle. Sees the novel as a
      brilliant tour de force and "an extra-ordinary amusing bur-
      lesque of the New England tradition." While "Leander steals
      the novel," Coverly and Moses are less ably drawn characters
      and cannot sustain the burden of a picaresque.

2 ANON. Review of The Wapshot Chronicle. Booklist 53 (1 June):
      500.
         Describes the novel as an "episodic, but cleverly written,
      narrative," which contains "a good deal of bawdy language."
      It is a formless but enjoyable novel.

3 ANON. Review of The Wapshot Chronicle. Virginia Kirkus Service
      25 (15 January): 50.
         Praises the sections of Leander's diary and the appearances
      of Honora for their "tart sting" and finds the novel as a whole
      "rowdy, bawdy, feeling, [and] root-sensed."

4 ANON. "Arts Body Elects 12 New Members." New York Times,
      2 February, p. 21.
         Reports Cheever's election to membership in the National
      Institute of Arts and Letters.

5 ANON. "Life in the Round." Times Literary Supplement 56
      (18 October): 621.
         Review of The Wapshot Chronicle. Praises Cheever for his
      "zest and vigour and sheer skill." Finds the novel bawdy and
      inventive, but contends that Cheever "is rather too insistently
      asking us to admire his self-conscious cleverness." Still,
      the book is full of delightful diversions, chief of which is
      Leander's autobiography.

6 ANON. "Notes on Current Books." Virginia Quarterly Review 33
      (Autumn): civ.
         Review of The Wapshot Chronicle. Finds the novel "some-
      what unresolved and tentative." While not dull, the work has
      "a rich, lingering quality of remembered puzzlement."

7 ANON. "Twilight for Leander." Time 69 (25 March): 112.
         Review of The Wapshot Chronicle. Praises the novel as
      "brilliantly written" and finds that it is "peppered with
      ribald good humor and peopled by some absurd zanies." Finds
      that Cheever has successfully made the transition from the
      short story to the larger scope of the novel.

8 BAKER, CARLOS. "Yankee Gallimaufry." Saturday Review 40
   (23 March): 14.
        Review of The Wapshot Chronicle. While parts of the novel
   reflect Cheever's short story strengths--the effective "limited
   scene, the separate episode, the overheard conversation, the
   crucial confrontation"--the book is not unified. This "gamy"
   novel reveals that Cheever can be wistful and touching, but
   that his forte is not architectonics. Reprinted: 1969.15.

9 BAYLEY, JOHN. "New Novels." The Spectator 199 (4 October):
   457-58.
        Review of The Wapshot Chronicle. Cheever gives the re-
   viewer "the feeling of something cold and watchful, something
   fundamentally not there." While he is as remorseless as Mary
   McCarthy in his examination of the "intimate side of life,"
   Cheever seems simultaneously attracted to it.

10 BRENNAN, MAEVE. "Mortal Men and Mermaids." New Yorker 33
   (11 May): 142, 144-46, 149-50.
        Review of The Wapshot Chronicle. Observes that Cheever's
   writing is a "celebration" and that this novel is "founded in
   his understanding of and joy in man's fruitfulness--in the
   enduring surge of the sexual instinct--and in his stony knowledge of his own mortality." Sees Cheever's genius at work in
   his study of Coverly and Moses, but finds that his portraits
   of many of the women are less detailed.

11 BURNS, JOHN A. Review of The Wapshot Chronicle. Library Journal
   82 (15 April): 1064.
        Finds this novel to be "beautifully written" and a "wonder-
   ful reading experience. Highly recommended."

12 BUTCHER, FANNY. "John Cheever Shows Great Skill in an Important
   First Novel." Chicago Sunday Tribune, 31 March, p. 4.
        Review of The Wapshot Chronicle. While confessing baffle-
   ment at the "episodic patternlessness" of this novel, the reviewer feels that this work "adds something new to the stream
   of American fiction." Praises Cheever's "ability to bring
   alive even a casual human shadow" and his facility for evok-
   ing mood, yet finds his sudden shifts of tone often confusing.

13 CASEY, GENEVIEVE M. Review of The Wapshot Chronicle. Books on
   Trial 15 (June-July): 453.
        Finds the novel, with its extremely thin plot, to be little
   more than "a series of highly polished episodes or character
   sketches." Cheever proves with this novel "that he lacks the
   constructive ability to move ahead from the almost too carefully wrought short story form of which he is a master."

1957

14 ESTY, WILLIAM. "Out of an Abundant Love of Created Things."
     <u>Commonweal</u> 66 (15 May): 187-88.
         Review of <u>The Wapshot Chronicle</u>. Finds this novel "wonder-
     ful to read" and praises Cheever's sensuous imagery in his
     descriptions of the sea and the trout lake. The novel reveals
     Cheever's awareness of loneliness and defeat in the world; yet
     it is tempered by the novelist's sophistication and gentle
     reassurance "of a fairy tale for grown ups." Reprinted
     1969.15.

15 GEISMAR, MAXWELL. "End of the Line." <u>New York Times Book Review</u>,
     24 March, p. 5.
         Review of <u>The Wapshot Chronicle</u>. Suspects that Cheever is
     attempting to "break loose" from the <u>New Yorker</u> "school" of
     fiction and views this novel as an entertaining work "which
     hovers on the edge of a more serious purpose." It is
     Cheever's concern with human loneliness and "the tragicomedy
     of sex" that heralds a break with the "proper confines of
     'sensibility' in the typical <u>New Yorker</u> story." Yet the book
     is too episodic to achieve "the inner growth and development
     of a novel." Reprinted: 1969.15.

16 H., R. F. "Rundown Family in Ancient Town." <u>Springfield Sunday
     Republican</u>, 26 May, p. 8-C.
         Review of <u>The Wapshot Chronicle</u>. Describes the novel as
     "nourishing fare in an era of rather undistinguished writing"
     and considers that "any New Englander whose youth is in the
     past" should be able to recognize some of those years in this
     book.

17 HUGHES, RILEY. Review of <u>The Wapshot Chronicle</u>. <u>Catholic World</u>
     185 (June): 232.
         Finds this "experimental" novel "arch, affected, morbid,
     unfunny, chaotic." Laments that the book is disconnected in
     plot and disjointed in style and that it is peopled with deca-
     dent characters out of Southern gothic fiction, transposed to
     New England.

18 KIRSCH, ROBERT R. "The Book Report." <u>Los Angeles Times</u>,
     3 April, Part III, p. 5.
         Review of <u>The Wapshot Chronicle</u>. Finds this novel "good-
     humored, bawdy, eccentric, colorful, honest, beautifully
     written," and having a "range of feeling and experimentation
     far beyond his short stories." Suggests that in its rambling,
     picaresque manner the novel has gone beyond the confines of
     <u>New Yorker</u> fiction.

19 KIRSCHTEN, ERNEST. "Twilight in New England." St. Louis Post-
    Dispatch, 28 April, p. 4-B.
        Review of The Wapshot Chronicle. Suggests that this novel
    may be "vaguely" called a prose Spoon River Anthology, for it
    does not "really wind up as a novel." Finds that the book is,
    in many respects, about women, but that they are Cheever's
    less successfully drawn characters. In all, the book's "parts
    are better than the whole," since Cheever intermittently suc-
    ceeds in capturing "big chunks" of life.

20 MacGILLIVRAY, ARTHUR. Review of The Wapshot Chronicle. Best
    Sellers 17 (1 April): 4-5.
        Finds that Cheever is more concerned with human nature than
    plot, relies on cliches, and has "what you would normally ex-
    pect from a New Yorker contributor--a firm satirical outlook."
    Because of his emphasis on loneliness and his vision of man as
    "ridiculous, pitiable," Cheever seems to be "a sad man."

21 MADDOCKS, MELVIN. "Cheever Tries a Novel." Christian Science
    Monitor, 28 March, p. 15.
        Review of The Wapshot Chronicle. Does not see the same
    level of sophistication and compassion that had characterized
    Cheever's earlier work. Finds that Cheever traces his pro-
    tagonists' decline "with style and gentle sadness" but fails
    "in a contrastingly coarse and imprudent way, with Moses and
    Coverly." Attributes this failure to the strain of "a short-
    story writer temporizing with the technical problems of a
    novel."

22 MALCOLM, DONALD. "John Cheever's Photograph Album." New
    Republic 136 (3 June): 17-18.
        Review of The Wapshot Chronicle. Finds that this highly
    episodic novel is held together by Cheever's "special view of
    life--a blend of gusto, nostalgia and profoundly innocent
    ribaldry that is unique to him." However, since various parts
    of the book are more memorable than the whole, Cheever's char-
    acters "shine in individual episodes, but seem to stagger at
    times under the burden of supporting a full-length novel."

23 MERLIN, MILTON. "Wapshot Chronicle is the First Novel by John
    Cheever." Los Angeles Times, 7 April, Part V, p. 8.
        Finds that this novel demonstrates Cheever's "wit, humor,
    warmth, insight and compassion," as well as his style, which
    is marked by "delicate beauty and lyricism." The book "pro-
    vides pleasures rare and rewarding."

24 PERRINE, LAURENCE. "Realism Plus Symbolism." Southwest Review
    42 (Spring): 166-67.

1957

> Review of <u>Stories</u>. Considers Cheever to be working "in the realistic tradition using symbolic overtones."

25 POORE, CHARLES. "Books of the Times." <u>New York Times</u>, 26 March, p. 31.
> Review of <u>The Wapshot Chronicle</u>. Describes the novel as "magnificently exuberant," enlivened by the presence of Leander, the "noblest and most rancid" character in the story. However, most of the novel's suspense lies in the unpredictability of matriarch Honora, a character "with a whim of iron."

26 SACHER, SUSAN. "New Creative Writers: 30 Novelists Whose First Work Appears this Season." <u>Library Journal</u> 82 (1 February): 431.
> Biographical note on Cheever, which mentions <u>The Way Some People Live</u> and <u>The Enormous Radio</u> and forecasts the March publication of <u>The Wapshot Chronicle</u>.

27 SCOTT, WINFIELD TOWNLEY. "John Cheever's Loving Comedy." <u>New York Herald Tribune Book Review</u>, 24 March, pp. 1, 9.
> Review of <u>The Wapshot Chronicle</u>. Enthusiastically praises Cheever for capturing the local color of St. Botolphs and finds that "New England atmospherics have not been so magically evoked since Sarah Orne Jewett wrote 'The Country of the Pointed Firs.'" Though the characterizations are all well handled, Cheever's "greatest success" is Leander. The novel, while at times becoming episodic, has a "richness of texture" that was written with love and not sentimentality; it is "a brilliant history."

28 STEVENSON, DAVID L. "Four Views of Love: New Fiction." <u>The Nation</u> 184 (13 April): 329.
> Review of <u>The Wapshot Chronicle</u>. Terms this "an adult entertainment" of loosely unified sketches that is generally an "aloof look at the fretful anxieties and the pleasant rewards of sex." Praises Cheever for treating sex in a cheerful, modern yet non-clinical manner.

1958

1 ANON. Review of <u>The Housebreaker of Shady Hill</u>. <u>Best Sellers</u> 18 (1 October): 253.
> Praises Cheever's "instinct for choosing the right details to limn setting and mood." Argues that despite the prior appearance of seven of the eight stories in the <u>New Yorker</u>, these pieces are not "typical" of that magazine, in the perjorative sense of "having no beginning, no end, but only middle." They are well developed and show that Cheever is a master of the genre.

2 ANON. Review of The Housebreaker of Shady Hill. Booklist 55
   (15 September): 46.
      Describes these stories as "sophisticated and smoothly
   written tales" that reflect the manners and problems of "the
   country-club set."

3 ANON. Review of The Housebreaker of Shady Hill. Virginia Kirkus
   Service 26 (1 July): 473.
      Finds that the world of these "suburbia-cum-nightmare"
   stories "is presented crisply, economically and with telling
   dispatch."

4 ANON. "Booksellers Cite 3 Writers' Works." New York Times,
   12 March, p. 26.
      Reports that The Wapshot Chronicle has won the National
   Book Award in fiction for 1958. The novel was cited by the
   judges "for candor and originality."

5 ANON. "Crack in the Picture Window." Time 72 (8 September):
   100, 102.
      Review of The Housebreaker of Shady Hill. Considers
   Cheever, after Marquand, to be "the ablest chronicler of the
   interior life of the organization man." Of these eight stories, "The Sorrows of Gin" is "the funniest and possibly the
   best in the book." All of the pieces, in their saturation
   with the details of suburban life, have a stunning impact on
   the reader "in the way that cotton carries chloroform."

6 FULLER, EDMUND. Man in Modern Fiction. New York: Random House,
   p. 79.
      Briefly mentions Cheever with Shirley Jackson and John
   Collier as writers who "have employed the demonic in their
   work, brilliantly though often relatively shallowly."

7 GILMAN, RICHARD. "Dante of Suburbia." Commonweal 69
   (19 December): 320.
      Review of The Housebreaker of Shady Hill. Cheever is the
   "Dante of the cocktail hour," and his most faithful, "well-
   heeled" readers masochistically enjoy each exposé he writes
   of their failed lives and loves. Thus much of the esteem for
   Cheever is based on psychological and not artistic foundations.
   Cheever himself is a sentimentalist prophet who, having called
   suburbia to repentance, finds deliverance in the wholesome,
   American pursuits of trout streams and softball. The adolescent values that Cheever depicts are ones he in fact shares.
   Thus, his Shady Hill stories may touch on sadness but cannot
   reach the level of real tragedy. Reprinted: 1969.15.

1958

8 HICKS, GRANVILLE. "Cheever and Others." Saturday Review 41
   (13 September): 33, 47.
         Review of The Housebreaker of Shady Hill. Finds that these
   stories are exciting in spite of the potentially dull subject
   matter of suburbia. In stories such as "The Country Husband"
   and the title story, Cheever is able to enter his characters'
   minds at the crucial moments of their vulnerability and at
   these times "shows his mastery." Reprinted: 1969.15.

9 KIRSCH, ROBERT R. "Cheever Paints Pallid Exurbia." Los Angeles
   Times, 21 September, Part V, p. 7.
         Review of The Housebreaker of Shady Hill. Finds that this
   collection is "one of the best examples of Cheever's gift of
   compression and characterization" and that it is Cheever's
   "unquestioned ability" that enables him to wring from the re-
   stricted world of Shady Hill "such depth and excitement."
   Still, it is time for Cheever to broaden his repertoire, as
   he has proved he can with The Wapshot Chronicle, and thus "say
   good-by to Shady Hill for a good long time."

10 McLAUGHLIN, RICHARD. "Cheever Stories of Suburban Life."
    Springfield Sunday Republican, 23 November, p. 6-D.
          Review of The Housebreaker of Shady Hill. Describes
    Cheever's treatment of his suburbanite "targets" as a shooting
    of "puckish, occasionally lethal darts" and finds that his
    humor is most successful when it is succinct.

11 McNAMARA, EUGENE. Review of The Housebreaker of Shady Hill.
    The Critic 17 (December-January): 59.
          Unlike the characters in The Enormous Radio who are "etched
    in vitriol," these characters have "softened with time."
    Praises Cheever for humanizing these well developed characters
    and for making us "see the individual struggling for recogni-
    tion under the impress of form" and contemporary regimentation.

12 MITGANG, HERBERT. "Books of the Times." New York Times,
    6 September, p. 15.
          Review of The Housebreaker of Shady Hill. Praises Cheever
    for his ability to look "at his people objectively," yet still
    see through them. Notes Cheever's "beautiful control" and
    tendency toward understatement, which stands in contrast to
    "the big statement . . . a Kay Boyle or an Irwin Shaw might
    make." Describes the collection as "a diagnosis of a particu-
    lar form of community life, at once striving and brave, melan-
    choly and humorous."

13 PEDEN, WILLIAM. "How Sad It All Is." New York Times Book Review,
    7 September, p. 5.

Review of <u>The Housebreaker of Shady Hill</u>. Considers
Cheever to be "one of the most urbane moralists of our times"
and finds the protagonist of the title story typical of
Cheever's characters, who "build their materialistically
successful lives upon extremely flimsy moral foundations."
Yet suggests that his preoccupation with the same type of
characters and situations may well be something Cheever "has
to fear."

14 SULLIVAN, RICHARD. "Eight Short Stories with Effect of Unity."
    <u>Chicago Sunday Tribune Magazine of Books</u>, 7 September, p. 2.
        Review of <u>The Housebreaker of Shady Hill</u>. Since these
    stories deal with the same kind of suburban people, the col-
    lection "produces an effect of full, thoro [sic] coverage of
    a given world of human experience." This "most admirably
    realized book" is marked by wit and control, and Cheever's
    prose "is both graceful and governed."

15 WATERMAN, ROLLENE. Biographical Sketch. <u>Saturday Review</u> 41
    (13 September): 33.
        Traces Cheever's life and includes Cheever's comments of
    the short story form and suburbia.

16 WERMUTH, PAUL C. Review of <u>The Housebreaker of Shady Hill</u>.
    <u>Library Journal</u> 83 (15 September): 2438-39.
        Finds that "these stories as a group have a different, and
    richer, effect than they do individually." As the "poet of
    the exurbs," Cheever tries to find meaning in the lives of his
    sad, lonely, and "not too bright" characters.

17 WICKENDEN, DAN. "Cheever Tales of Suburbia." <u>New York Herald
    Tribune Book Review</u>, 7 September, p. 5.
        Review of <u>The Housebreaker of Shady Hill</u>. Notes that
    Cheever approaches his subject "as a compassionate ironist,"
    so that even in suburbia "magic occasionally shimmers." Finds
    that many of his characters seem sad, yet "more fully alive
    than the people in current fiction tend to be."

<u>1959</u>

1 HOWE, IRVING. "Realities and Fictions." <u>Partisan Review</u> 26
   (Winter): 130-31.
       Review of <u>The Housebreaker of Shady Hill</u>. Labels Cheever
   "a toothless Thurber" who "connives in the cowardice of contemporary life." Finds that Cheever "systematically refuses
   to face the meaning of the material he has himself brought to
   awareness and then suppressed." Cheever does not permit his
   characters to face defeat with either desperation or dignity.

1959

2 HUGHES, RILEY. Review of The Housebreaker of Shady Hill.
      Catholic World 189 (July): 325–26.
         Finds that most of the characters in this collection share
      the common buffer of money. These stories seem to state that
      "there can be no tragedy . . . if one changes one's illusions,
      if one accepts, or surrenders." Furthermore, there seems to
      be some "mockery" on Cheever's part "toward the characters he
      has lightly, delicately flayed."

3 SHRAPNEL, NORMAN. "The Retreat from Style." Manchester Guardian,
      30 January, p. 6.
         Review of The Housebreaker of Shady Hill. Maintains that
      unlike "typical" New Yorker fiction's "loaded irony," which is
      the product of a "concoctor's not an artist's method,"
      Cheever's stories are intense and written with "uncommon
      vitality." Notes also that Cheever's work, in its "essential
      seriousness," may well be the prose equivalent of John
      Betjeman's poetry.

4 TUCKER, MARTIN. "A Pluralistic Place." Venture 3: 69–73.
         Review of The Housebreaker of Shady Hill. While Cheever
      is "never sentimental" in this collection, his stories tend
      to be contrived. By endowing his heroes with "the saving
      grace of humor and tolerance," Cheever limits the significance
      of their situations. His preference for self-satisfied charac-
      ters instead of "dreary, confused people" has possibly "cut
      off larger issues of humanity."

1960

1 G[INGRICH], A[RNOLD]. "This Month In San Francisco: The Third
      Esquire Symposium." Esquire 54 (October): 6.
         Report on Esquire's "Writing in America Today" symposium,
      at which Cheever was one of three panelists. Mentions
      Cheever's literary career briefly.

2 GUTWILLIG, ROBERT. "Dim Views Through Fog." New York Times
      Book Review, 13 November, pp. 68–69.
         Reports that Cheever concluded his principal speech at the
      Esquire symposium by noting that the "only position for a
      writer now is negation."

1961

1 ADAMS, PHOEBE. "Potpouri." Atlantic Monthly 207 (June): 106.
         Review of Some People, Places and Things That Will Not
      Appear in My Next Novel. Despite their variety, finds these
      stories unified by the author's "silk-smooth, deceptively

conversational style" and by a point of view "that may best be
described as well-mannered fury."

2 ANON. Review of Some People, Places, and Things That Will Not
   Appear in My Next Novel. Booklist 57 (1 June): 606.
       Finds that Cheever's concern for modern man is reflected in
   this collection's "humor, irony, poignancy and other emotional
   states."

3 ANON. Review of Some People, Places, and Things That Will Not
   Appear in My Next Novel. Virginia Kirkus Service 29
   (1 February): 128.
       Describes this collection as ranging from "the stinging to
   the bleak." Finds that Cheever underscores "modern chaos,
   sometimes with terror, sometimes with pity."

4 ANON. "Fiction." The Bookmark 20 (April–May): 169.
       Review of Some People, Places, and Things That Will Not
   Appear in My Next Novel. Mentions the publication of these
   "lucid, original, sophisticated" stories.

5 ANON. "Into the Light." Newsweek 57 (1 May): 100.
       Review of Some People, Places, and Things That Will Not
   Appear in My Next Novel. Finds this collection "fascinating"
   and considers Cheever to be a "poetic writer, infused with a
   sense of the range and beauty of the natural world, the com-
   plexity and wonder of human personality and imagination."
   Also paraphrases Cheever's comments on the "'largeness' of
   great literature," in which he discusses Dostoevski, Proust,
   and Joyce and their "moral intensity."

6 ANON. "New Fiction." Times (London), 3 August, p. 11.
       Review of Some People, Places, and Things That Will Not
   Appear in My Next Novel. Places these stories in "the school
   of highbrow Americana" and finds that, despite the efforts of
   the publisher to make them seem pretentious, these pieces are
   all "elegantly turned and several of them have neat points at
   the end."

7 ANON. "Notes on Current Books." Virginia Quarterly Review 37
   (Autumn): cxviii.
       Review of Some People, Places, and Things That Will Not
   Appear in My Next Novel. Finds that these "urbane and brittle
   sketches" describe characters and situations which the reviewer hopes "will trouble him [Cheever] enough to become
   revenants."

1961

8 ANON. "One Man's Hell." Time 77 (28 April): 103-4.
      Review of Some People, Places, and Things That Will Not
   Appear in My Next Novel. Hopes that "the title is accurate,"
   because Cheever "is in danger of getting bogged down in his
   talent-lined rut." Finds that in his depictions of hell, "The
   Death of Justina" is more explicit than "Brimmer" or "The
   Scarlet Moving Van" and that in his stories set abroad,
   Cheever "seems to find a new freedom," having "thrown away
   the guidebook."

9 ANON. "Other New Novels." Times Literary Supplement 60
      (4 August): 477.
      Review of Some People, Places, and Things That Will Not
   Appear in My Next Novel. Praises these stories for "their
   graphic style, their firm judgment and an all-resourceful
   humour."

10 BARO, GENE. "Mr. Cheever's Sleights-of-Mood Performed with Con-
      summate Skill." New York Herald Tribune Lively Arts and Book
      Review, 30 April, p. 29.
      Review of Some People, Places, and Things That Will Not
   Appear in My Next Novel. Although Cheever is a skilled
   writer, "his work lacks intellectual passion or an enlarged
   vision of reality." Describes Cheever as a virtuoso stylist
   who uses irony and reversal as "an intricate trick"; however,
   this does not compel a "greater understanding of ourselves."

11 BOROFF, DAVID. "A World Filled with Trapdoors Into Chaos." New
      York Times Book Review, 16 April, p. 34.
      Review of Some People, Places, and Things That Will Not
   Appear in My Next Novel. Sees Cheever as "a Gothic writer
   whose mind is poised at the edge of terror." Finds that "The
   Death of Justina" embodies the leitmotif of Cheever's work
   and that with the exception of "The Golden Age" and the title
   piece, Cheever "restores mystery and joy and even a bewildered
   grandeur" to contemporary literature.

12 CAREW, JAN. "Spiritual Suburbs." Time and Tide 42 (10 August):
      1323.
      Review of Some People, Places, and Things That Will Not
   Appear in My Next Novel. Terms these stories "sophisticated
   and neatly tailored" but faults Cheever for his "elegant mannerisms" and "manipulations of style," which result in a lack
   of "passion, energy and insight."

13 CHAMBERLAIN, JOHN. "One Last Asset." Wall Street Journal,
      1 May, p. 10.

Review of Some People, Places, and Things That Will Not
Appear in My Next Novel. Contends that although Cheever is "a
first-rate artist in atmospheric prose," his writing has suf-
fered from the constraints imposed by "the latter-day magazine
formula that insists on little sad tales about little sad
people." Notes also that Cheever's dry irony is well suited
for treating the sort of characters and situations he has re-
solved to eliminate.

14 CRUTTWELL, PATRICK. "Fiction Chronicle." The Hudson Review 14
(Autumn): 448-54.
Review of Some People, Places, and Things That Will Not
Appear in My Next Novel. Describes this collection as "admi-
rably readable," although most of the stories are variations
on one theme: the nightmare that exists behind the American
dream.

15 DIDION, JOAN. "A Celebration of Life." National Review 10
(22 April): 254-55.
Review of Some People, Places, and Things That Will Not
Appear in My Next Novel. Sees Cheever as a "chronicler of a
world . . . caught in the ruins of a particular stratum of
American society that somewhere along the way, probably during
the 1920s, lost its will." Finds that his concern for detail
"leads him down roads he cannot possibly follow, into cul-de-
sacs . . . that do not, finally, interest him."

16 FADIMAN, CLIFTON. "Reading I've Liked." Holiday 30 (August):
23.
Review of Some People, Places, and Things That Will Not
Appear in My Next Novel. Finds this collection intelligent
in its depiction of "our gentler 'civilized' class" in times
of isolation and alienation.

17 GOLD, HERBERT and STEVENSON, DAVID L. "Editors' Analysis." In
Stories of Modern America, p. 193. New York: St. Martin's
Press.
Analysis of "The Country Husband." Sees the protagonist
at the end of the story as "perhaps sadder, and if not wiser
then at least chastened." Followed by five review questions.
Reprinted: 1967.4.

18 HASSAN, IHAB. Radical Innocence: Studies in the Contemporary
American Novel. Princeton: Princeton University Press,
pp. 109, 188-94, 200-201, 331.
Focuses primarily on The Wapshot Chronicle and finds that
this novel shows "life to be at worst a kind of whimsical
Puritan purgatory." The world of this novel is a metaphor

1961

"created by style," where "myth tends to assume the guise of romance, and comedy borrows the spirit of fantasy." Cheever avoids any exploration of his myth and so plot, structure, and characterization all become secondary to style, which he prefers to use to sustain his affirmative vision of life. Reprinted: 1973.17.

19 HOGAN, WILLIAM. "Some Inhabitants of Cheever Country." San Francisco Chronicle, 28 April, p. 35.
    Review of Some People, Places, and Things That Will Not Appear in My Next Novel. Describes this collection as a "showcase" for Cheever's talent of observation of "mid-century American frustration." Finds that Cheever's vision of modern life as "a modern Dante's Inferno at best" is a bleak one.

20 HUTCHENS, JOHN K. "Some People, Places . . . " New York Herald Tribune, 28 April, p. 21.
    Review of Some People, Places, and Things That Will Not Appear in My Next Novel. Compares Cheever's writing to the efforts of "a fine athlete," because it is graceful, strong, and "a minimum of strain is visible." Finds that this collection, in its range of "tenderness and terror, irony and love," reveals a "mature and intelligent" artist's view of life.

21 JOHNSON, CHARLES W. Review of Some People, Places, and Things That Will Not Appear in My Next Novel. The Critic 19 (June-July): 21-22.
    Praises Cheever's "constancy" of style and finds the stories "slick, but compassionate and often wryly ironic." Describes the characters as "interesting to meet."

22 KAPP, ISA. "Confession of a Writer." New Leader 44 (18 September): 29-30.
    Review of Some People, Places, and Things That Will Not Appear in My Next Novel. Finds that while "The Duchess" is the best story in the collection, "The Lowboy" embodies the major theme of the book: a writer should discard "those useless relics of his past which obsess him and limit his imagination." Feels that Cheever's writing to date has been in "too narrow a space between the original grey Cheever and his lyrical opposing self" and hopes that his future work will benefit from this collection's literary exorcism.

23 KIRSCH, ROBERT R. "Cheever Declares Independence." Los Angeles Times, 6 April, Part III, p. 5.
    Review of Some People, Places, and Things That Will Not Appear in My Next Novel. Contends that Cheever has been in "transition" since The Wapshot Chronicle and that these

stories reflect this phase of his career. Cheever has grown beyond the reportage of the "circumscribed world of the New Yorker," and his observations now have "added dimension and depth."

24 LAUT, STEPHEN J. Review of Some People, Places, and Things That Will Not Appear in My Next Novel. Best Sellers 21 (15 May): 83.

These stories, like most of Cheever's work, "seem slick and realistic on the surface, but beneath there is always a great impacted mass meaning." Praises the use of allegory in "The Death of Justina" and Cheever's "apt use of literary short-hand" in "Brimmer," among others noted, yet concludes that none of these pieces is "really memorable." Because the work is "clever and cerebral" and the characters are "like bugs under a microscope," one is fascinated but rarely involved.

25 McGUINNESS, FRANK. "Some People, Places and Things That Need Scarcely Appear Anywhere." New Statesman 62 (4 August): 161.

Review of Some People, Places, and Things That Will Not Appear in My Next Novel. Labels the collection "a sad dis-appointment." Finds that these stories alternate between being slick, clever, and whimsical.

26 MADDOCKS, MELVIN. "Cheever's Latest Collection." Christian Science Monitor, 4 May, p. 11.

Review of Some People, Places, and Things That Will Not Appear in My Next Novel. Finds that Cheever's "intensity and compassion" for his subjects set him apart from other New Yorker writers and notes that Cheever writes "as if Marquand had somehow been crossed with Kafka, and the standard New Yorker flavor of a twist of lemon suddenly interrupted by a mouthful of ashes." It is evident that Cheever is "a writer of formidable equipment."

27 MITCHELL, JULIAN. "Old Hat Re-Blocked." The Spectator 207 (11 August): 210.

Review of Some People, Places, and Things That Will Not Appear in My Next Novel. Describes this collection as "a serious book by a writer deeply concerned with his craft." While a number of the stories are funny, Cheever remains compassionate throughout. "The Death of Justina" is termed "particularly good."

28 POORE, CHARLES. "Books of the Times." New York Times, 16 May, p. 35.

Review of Some People, Places, and Things That Will Not Appear in My Next Novel. Dismisses as "acid malarkey"

1961

Cheever's claim that this collection will enable him to exorcise certain character types from his future writing and finds
that these stories are "a pleasure to read." Notes that
Cheever avoids repeating himself throughout, with the possible
exception of "a Jamesian fondness for writing about Americans
in Italy."

29 PRICE, R. G. G. "New Fiction." Punch 241 (9 August): 223-24.
Review of Some People, Places, and Things That Will Not
Appear in My Next Novel. Since these stories are not really
about anything, they make one "long . . . for meat rather than
sauce." Cheever here has prepared a "dazzling display of how
to cook left-overs," and this collection stands in sharp contrast to The Wapshot Chronicle, which revealed Cheever's "pas-
sionate concern for subject-matter."

30 QUIGLY, ISABEL. "Voting with the Soul." Manchester Guardian,
28 July, p. 7.
Review of Some People, Places, and Things That Will Not
Appear in My Next Novel. Finds this collection "charming"
and "immensely readable" and notes that all the pieces are
informed with "the same brand of sweet-sour predictable
melancholy."

31 RAY, DAVID. "The Weeding-Out Process." Saturday Review 44
(27 May): 20.
Review of Some People, Places, and Things That Will Not
Appear in My Next Novel. Views this book as the search of
"an enlightened Puritan" for aesthetic discipline and at the
same time as a work of fiction that dramatizes "modern man's
search for order." In its treatment of both of them, this
book is a work "of the first magnitude."

32 SHERMAN, THOMAS B. "Reading and Writing: John Cheever's Pleas-
ing Gifts as a Satirist." St. Louis Post-Dispatch, 21 May,
p. 4-B.
Review of Some People, Places, and Things That Will Not
Appear in My Next Novel. Finds that Cheever's writing is
"mildly ironic, mildly compassionate," and that he has the
"charm that makes this easy-going, uneventful kind of narration engaging." Notes also that some of the pieces in this
book are New Yorker-style stories: "They seem to be complete
stories which have been chopped off at both ends."

33 SULLIVAN, RICHARD. "Concern, Control, and Grace on Every Page."
Chicago Sunday Tribune Magazine of Books, 30 April, p. 3.
Review of Some People, Places, and Things That Will Not
Appear in My Next Novel. Considers all of these stories

"quiet and distinguished works of art in fiction." Finds that
Cheever deals with "real and human" concerns with an "essay-
ist's touch" and avoids melodrama. His prose is "skilled,
accomplished, finished," and his approach is "thoughtful,
even meditative."

34 WALBRIDGE, EARLE F. "WLB Biography: John Cheever." Wilson
Library Bulletin 36 (December): 324.
Recounts Cheever's biographical data and traces his literary career from 1930 to 1961. Includes excerpts from representative reviews of his work.

35 WARNKE, FRANK J. "Cheever's Inferno." New Republic 144
(15 May): 18.
Review of Some People, Places, and Things That Will Not
Appear in My Next Novel. Notes that Cheever's "vision is
more nightmare than promise, and his struggle against the
terms of his vision has made this book less than what it might
have been." Thus "The Death of Justina" and "Brimmer" suc-
ceed, while "The Wrysons" and even "Boy in Rome" are marked
by a "failure of nerve." Still, Cheever is a master stylist
and, to a degree, comparable to Hawthorne and Melville, where
"he is a haunted chronicler of the impingements of an inexplicable malevolence on ordinary life," and to Hawthorne and
James, where "he is obsessed by the contrast between American
rawness and innocence and European culture and experience."

36 WERMUTH, PAUL C. Review of Some People, Places, and Things That
Will Not Appear in My Next Novel. Library Journal 86
(15 April): 1618.
Finds that these are good stories but that the style
"strains a bit for poetic effects." Notes that the Italian
settings of some of the pieces "seem a new element in the
author's work, but not a vital one."

1962

1 HERZBERG, MAX J., ed. The Reader's Encyclopedia of American
Literature. New York: Thomas Y. Crowell, p. 169.
Provides brief biographical data and lists Cheever's works
published through 1961. Erroneously notes that Cheever received two Guggenheim Fellowships.

2 KAZIN, ALFRED. Contemporaries. Boston: Little, Brown,
pp. 214-15.
Finds that although Salinger's characters are "larger and
more human" than Cheever's, the latter "has the gift for being
more detached and at the same time more open" to the dangers

of experience. Notes that too often Cheever is a "slyer John
O'Hara," since he tends to fall into "mechanical habits of
documentation." Reprinted: 1969.28.

1963

1 ANON. "John Cheever." Celebrity Register. New York: Harper &
   Row, p. 116.
       Brief biographical notice with an excerpt from Some People,
   Places, and Things That Will Not Appear in My Next Novel.

2 BRACHER, FREDERICK. "John Cheever and Comedy." Critique:
   Studies in Modern Fiction 6 (Spring): 66-77.
       Argues that in his short stories and The Wapshot Chronicle,
   Cheever writes in the comic mode, in the classic sense: he
   is concerned with man's possibilities rather than his limitations. Cheever's fiction makes clear that "the man who
   accepts initiatory pain is rewarded by the capacity for
   beauty, a sense of freedom, and the power of love." Notes
   that the flat characterization and the frequent absence of
   traditional plot are consequences of Cheever's greater concern for "sequences of feeling" than for conventional fictional structure. Reprinted: 1973.32.

1964

1 ALDRIDGE, JOHN W. "Where Life is But a Dream-World." New York
   Herald Tribune Book Week, 25 October, pp. 3, 19.
       Review of The Brigadier and the Golf Widow. Contends
   that despite Cheever's many distinguished stories, "his
   breakthrough into genuine excellence and serious reputation"
   has been obstructed by the "too coy and cloying" effect of
   the "nightmare trivialities" in his writing. Laments Cheever's
   tendency to absorb all of the "discordant extremes of conduct
   and perception" into a New Yorker-style, "fundamentally
   equable view of life." Sees Cheever's occasional use of
   "grotesqueries" as a result of his desire "to be taken seriously" and finds a number of the pieces in this collection
   "uneven" and even "mechanical." Concludes that Cheever "does
   not yet disturb us enough." Reprinted: 1966.1; 1972.1;
   1975.4.

2 ANON. Review of The Brigadier and the Golf Widow. Booklist 61
   (1 November): 248.
       Cheever is again "impressive as stylist and psychologist."
   He maintains his control of mood and emotion throughout.

3 ANON. Review of <u>The Brigadier and the Golf Widow</u>. <u>Choice</u> 1
     (December): 421.
          Finds these stories comparable to Thurber's and John
     Collier's, "for here is the eery in the midst of suburban
     normality, the hidden terror of seemingly normal people."

4 ANON. Review of <u>The Wapshot Scandal</u>. <u>Booklist</u> 60
     (1 February): 488.·
          As in <u>The Wapshot Chronicle</u>, Cheever again is successful
     in the environment of St. Botolphs. The contrasts he draws
     between past and present are both memorable and "highly
     perceptive."

5 ANON. Review of <u>The Wapshot Scandal</u>. <u>Choice</u> 1 (March): 21.
          Praises Cheever's "ability to reveal touching tragedy in
     the midst of wildly improbable events." Finds Cheever a
     master chronicler of daily, incessant frustrations.

6 ANON. "Cheever to Visit Soviet." <u>New York Times</u>, 29 September,
     p. 34.
          Reports Cheever's planned visit to the Soviet Union, West
     Germany, and Italy.

7 ANON. "The Chill of the Times." <u>Newsweek</u> 64 (30 November):
     104-5.
          Review of <u>The Brigadier and the Golf Widow</u>. Compares
     Cheever to John O'Hara "in outlook and setting" and to Scott
     Fitzgerald on "the more poetic and romantic" side. Still,
     Cheever's sensibility seems, at times, "so weird that it
     veers perilously close to Charles Addams."

8 ANON. "Edge of Darkness." <u>Time</u> 84 (16 October): 121.
          Review of <u>The Brigadier and the Golf Widow</u>. Finds "The
     Swimmer" to be typical of one of Cheever's preoccupations:
     "the prosperous suburbanite who turns an unsuspecting corner
     and falls off the edge of things into outer darkness." Com-
     pares Cheever to Kafka and finds that Cheever writes of the
     more subtle terror of "citizens richly and pointlessly re-
     warded by an equally faceless society."

9 ANON. "The Ghost of Chicsville." <u>Time</u> 83 (24 January): 68, 70.
          Review of <u>The Wapshot Scandal</u>. Calling Cheever "one of the
     most curious and original writers in the U.S. today," the
     reviewer sees him as "an old-fashioned moralist" and as the
     "first poet-mythologist" of suburbia. This novel dramatizes,
     through the lives of Moses and Coverly, two basic themes that
     are recurrent in American literature: "the Desirable Life and
     the Lost Innocence of men looking wistfully back on a

1964

small-town and country boyhood." The result is an "enigmatic
and gruesome fable . . . by a writer who is not yet great,
but who is greatly obsessed by his exploration of American
life."

10 ANON. "New Fiction." Times (London), 10 September, p. 15.
Review of The Wapshot Scandal. Sees the novel as a "disappointing" sequel to The Wapshot Chronicle. It seems
strained and long, and Cheever's "hot, wet breath is in one's
ear, whispering continuously" and prevents adequate character
development.

11 ANON. "Notes on Current Books." Virginia Quarterly Review 40
(Spring): lvi.
Review of The Wapshot Scandal. Faults Cheever's use of
picaresque methods and finds that the characters "have run
away with his book." Also his various points of view have
only "tangential concern . . . with the main business of the
novel."

12 ANON. "St. Botolphs' Saga." Newsweek 63 (13 January): 76.
Review of The Wapshot Scandal. Finds the novel "excursive"
rather than "episodic" and praises the "extraordinary depth
of character" and Cheever's "real feel for the fabric of
society." Notes that Emile's involvement in the egg hunt
becomes a suburban version of The Day of the Locust and
finds that this "chilling and hilarious book" ends on "perhaps an echo of hope."

13 ANON. "Wapshot Agonies." Times Literary Supplement 63
(10 September): 838.
Review of The Wapshot Scandal. Despite Cheever's occasional exuberance, this novel has a generally sad tone, for
Cheever seems to say that modern life is too complicated for
people to cope with. The novel is somewhat reminiscent of
Under Milk Wood in its romantic rhetoric, and it is "most
acceptable as a series of good stories, even good jokes,"
than as a serious philosophical account of the agony of contemporary man.

14 BARRETT, WILLIAM. "New England Gothic." Atlantic Monthly 213
(February): 140.
Review of The Wapshot Scandal. Unlike J. P. Marquand,
Cheever is a social moralist who is also a "visionary," with
an imagination that goes beyond realism into the fantastic
and the grotesque. This is a powerful if uneven novel by a
latter-day Hawthorne, although his "vision of evil is too
immense" to be adequately manifest in the Wapshots.

15 BRACHER, FREDERICK. "John Cheever: A Vision of the World."
    Claremont Quarterly 11 (Winter): 47-57.
        Views Cheever as one of "our most significant writers of
    comedy," with an ability "to catch the ephemeral quality and
    feel of life in a period of accelerating change." Discusses
    the development of Cheever's vision from his first story col-
    lection through The Wapshot Scandal, noting that while the
    original "wry wit persists," it is increasingly tempered by
    humor and warmth. Finds that his books Some People, Places,
    and Things That Will Not Appear in My Next Novel and The
    Wapshot Scandal are "more somber in tone and more critical
    of our mechanized civilization;" yet all of Cheever's writing
    is characterized by "moral earnestness." Bracher then focuses
    on four recent stories, "Bella Lingua," "Events of That
    Easter," "A Vision of the World," and "The Embarkment for
    Cythera" to illustrate that Cheever's fiction has moved from
    social comedy to "deeper levels." Reprinted: 1973.32.

16 BRICKER, RICHARD P. "Other New Books to Know About." Book-of-
    the-Month Club News, October, p. 13.
        Review of The Brigadier and the Golf Widow. Notes that
    most of these stories deal with "modern man's casual capacity
    for brutal destruction." Finds that the collection is in-
    formed by Cheever's "highly flexible imagination, an unsen-
    timental sense of horror and a rueful sense of humor."

17 BUNKER, PATRICIA. "Fall Kicks Off the Big Book." Saturday
    Review 47 (3 October): 38.
        Notice of The Brigadier and the Golf Widow. Sees this
    collection as having "16 more fanciful reasons why Mr. Cheever
    stands tall among short-story writers."

18 CORKE, HILARY. "Sugary Days in Saint Botolphs." New Republic
    150 (25 January): 19-21.
        Review of The Wapshot Scandal. Although this material was
    enjoyable when it appeared in segments in the New Yorker, in
    novel form it is "fatally flawed" by "carelessnesses and
    loosenesses of construction" and by Cheever's "bouts of
    arrant sentimentality." Finds that the novel is a compila-
    tion of "contradictory episodes" connected "with decorative
    tinsel." Many of the scenes, such as Coverly's rescue of his
    brother on Christmas Eve, "might have made Dickens, at his
    absurdest, pause and blush." Reprinted: 1972.3; 1975.5.

19 CORMIER, ROBERT. Review of The Wapshot Chronicle. The Sign 43
    (March): 63-64.
        Praises Cheever as "one of the ablest writers of the day,"
    even though his "novel is never quite a novel." That the

1964

characters are virtually captives of a set of unpleasant cir-
cumstances does not prevent Cheever's "grace and wit" from
making a potentially tragic story into an entertaining one.

20 CREWS, FREDERICK C. "Domestic Manners." New York Review of
    Books, 22 October, pp. 7-8.
        Review of The Brigadier and the Golf Widow. Notes that
    Cheever is "a remarkably serene writer who has always been
    at home with his cast of wealthy neurotics and petty adven-
    turers," and in this collection the only change is that these
    characters are older and "more entrenched in the suburban
    code." Finds that although Cheever "celebrates his charac-
    ters' banality," these stories often lack "sincerity and
    psychological interest."

21 DeMOTT, BENJAMIN. "The Way We Feel Now." Harper's 228
    (February): 111-12.
        Review of The Wapshot Scandal. Finds this sequel to the
    Chronicle--Cheever's "best book"--to be episodic, yet an in-
    telligent and witty examination of modern life as "living
    hell." Cheever combines "remarkable comic inventiveness"
    with the wry stance of a social psychologist to produce a
    novel of pathos. But among the book's limitations is its
    inherent obsolescence, due to Cheever's reliance on contem-
    porary allusions and the abbreviated range of his feeling,
    which is often little more than "a generalizing pity for
    human helplessness." Reprinted: 1969.15.

22 DIDION, JOAN. "The Way We Live Now." National Review 16
    (24 March): 237-38, 240.
        Review of The Wapshot Scandal. Considers this novel to be
    another version of the "one great story" Cheever has been
    telling throughout his career: the tale of once happy chil-
    dren "led astray by natural error and inflexibly punished,
    banished from the Eden that lies all around us." Cheever's
    characters then "love life the more because they so fear
    death." Concludes that "no other writer today . . . tells
    us so much about the way we live now."

23 DOLBIER, MAURICE. "Jabberwocks and Snarks." New York Herald
    Tribune, 14 October, p. 27.
        Review of The Brigadier and the Golf Widow. Finds that in
    this collection Cheever adds a dimension of Lewis Carroll to
    the city and suburbs "we think we know." In most of these
    pieces, which number among Cheever's best work, there is a
    blend of "farce and feeling, irrelevancies and universals."

24 FADIMAN, CLIFTON. "Other New Books to Know About." Book-of-the-
Month Club News, January, p. 11.
Review of The Wapshot Scandal. Describes the novel as "dis-
concerting, diffuse yet oddly fascinating." It seems part
realism, part melodrama, and part fantasy, due to "a whimsical
alternation in tone," and the reader is left "in a state of
interesting suspension" at the end.

25 FRANCOEUR, ROBERT A. Review of The Brigadier and the Golf Widow.
Best Sellers 24 (15 December): 379, 384.
Notes that these stories often concern sexual obsession and
sadness and that Cheever's sarcasm is tempered "by the sincer-
ity of his concern for human problems." "Reunion" and "The
Angel of the Bridge" stand out from the rest "because of the
disparity of sentiments that they effectively dramatize."

26 FULLER, EDMUND. "Cheever's America." Wall Street Journal,
28 January, p. 10.
Review of The Wapshot Scandal. While this uneven novel is
a disappointing sequel to The Wapshot Chronicle, it is still
a "disquieting" novel. Through it Cheever views modern life
"with a wry disenchantment."

27 GARRETT, GEORGE. "John Cheever and the Charms of Innocence:
The Craft of The Wapshot Scandal." Hollins Critic 1
(April): 1-4, 6-12.
Suggests that with the publication of The Wapshot Scandal,
Cheever has become "a major writer." Explains how Cheever
altered the form of the classic New Yorker story after World
War II. Sees the relationship between the two Wapshot novels
as similar to that of Faulkner's The Hamlet and The Town, in
that Cheever's two novels are his "old testament, written of
the time of myths, the law of the prophets." Notes that The
Wapshot Scandal, with its concluding Christian statement, is
Cheever's "most ambitious work and his finest achievement."
Reprinted: 1971.3; 1973.32; 1975.4.

28 GRAU, SHIRLEY ANN. "New and Noteworthy." Cosmopolitan 156
(January): 28-29.
Review of The Wapshot Scandal. Finds the novel "equally
divided between genius and nonsense." Argues that Melissa is
the most interesting of the Wapshot family, since we empathize
with her efforts to carry on an affair with the grocery boy.
Still, despite all its cleverness, the novel is contrived, and
Cheever "has allowed the scandal to turn to silliness."

29 GRAUEL, GEORGE E. Review of The Wapshot Scandal. Best Sellers
23 (15 January): 363.

1964

Finds that the episodic quality of the work makes it more
"an Our Town collection of short stories" than a unified novel.
The book is unpredictable and ranges from realism to satire to
"benign good humor." Through it all, Cheever provokes reflection "without incurring an inartistic didacticism."

30 GREENE, GEORGE. "From Christmas to Christmas--A Ramble with the
    Wapshots." Commonweal 79 (24 January): 487-88.
        Review of The Wapshot Scandal. Because of the attention
    Cheever pays to Coverly, the book should have been entitled
    "'The Education of Coverly Wapshot.'" This novel sharply
    verifies the American passion of loneliness and sin of impa-
    tience more effectively than any recent novel, and Cheever's
    dialogue is so successful that it is able to "expose like an
    x-ray."

31 HARDWICK, ELIZABETH. "The Family Way." New York Review of Books,
    6 February, pp. 4-5.
        Review of The Wapshot Scandal. Contends that Cheever "at
    his best is given to suffering, not satire," and for that
    reason his stories in The Enormous Radio are most memorable.
    In the Wapshot novels, however, sentimentality and "unavoid-
    able bits of Our-Townism deform the style," and Cheever
    strains to convey, in his characterization of the elder
    Wapshots, "a form of moral beauty not based upon deed so
    much as upon a certain casual charm of manner." Suggests
    also that Cheever's master is probably F. Scott Fitzgerald
    and his disciple is John Updike.

32 HICKS, GRANVILLE. "Slices of Life in An Age of Anxiety."
    Saturday Review 47 (17 October): 33.
        Review of The Brigadier and the Golf Widow. Describes
    Cheever as "the chronicler of life in upper-middle-class
    suburbia in the Age of Anxiety" and praises him for his
    terse and pointed stories. Finds "Metamorphoses" not as
    successful as the other pieces, but sees "The Angel of the
    Bridge" as one of the best, in which the reader is never
    informed of his destination until he reaches it. This col-
    lection reveals that Cheever "is as good as ever and maybe a
    little better."

33 _____. "Where Have All the Roses Gone?" Saturday Review 47
    (4 January): 75-76.
        Review of The Wapshot Scandal. Sees the novel as a vigor-
    ous narrative, yet having an elegiac tone. Praises Cheever's
    poignant concern for modern man's loss of dignity and main-
    tains that Cheever "writes about the special perils of the
    moment with extraordinary effectiveness."

34 _____. "The World as We Want It." Saturday Review 47
(25 January): 27-28.
Discusses the virtues and defects of technological progress
and alludes to The Wapshot Scandal to illustrate how individuals have now lost the sort of "support that membership in a
community once provided."

35 HIGGINSON, JEANNETTE. "Recent Novels." Minnesota Review 4
(Spring): 450, 452-54.
Review of The Wapshot Scandal. Notes that this novel is a
"worthy sequel" to The Wapshot Chronicle, and like its predecessor, The Wapshot Scandal is "episodic (yet never diffuse)."
Praises Cheever for his "boisterous sense of farce, a severe
appreciation of moral tragedy, and an unusual understanding of
people as individuals with potentialities of goodness and
happiness."

36 HYMAN, STANLEY EDGAR. "John Cheever's Golden Egg." New Leader
47 (3 February): 23-24.
Review of The Wapshot Scandal. Argues that as with his
first novel, Cheever here has tried and failed "to make short
story material jell as a novel." This is due largely to a
lack of unity and an "inconsistency of character and tone."
Yet much of the book is "extremely funny" and often results
in effective satire, thus making this book "a very impressive
non-novel." Reprinted: 1966.5.

37 JANEWAY, ELIZABETH. "Things Aren't What They Seem." New York
Times Book Review, 5 January, pp. 1, 28.
Review of The Wapshot Scandal. Finds that Cheever uses a
number of diverse myths "brilliantly and energetically" in
this novel and that more than any modern writer except
Nabokov, he uses the features of contemporary life "for the
purposes of art." Describes the twists the novel takes as
"rich and tricky and full of surprises."

38 JOHNSON, LUCY. "Out of the Past." The Progressive 28 (April):
42-43.
Review of The Wapshot Scandal. Praises Cheever for his
"fabulous imagination" and finds the novel well plotted and
suspenseful, combining "inventiveness, compassion, and a wild
(and sometimes low) humor."

39 KAY, JANE H. "Cheever's Gift for the Ordinary." Christian
Science Monitor, 22 October, p. 7.
Review of The Brigadier and the Golf Widow. Despite a
tendency toward stagey simplicity, Cheever's special skill is
his ability "to make us one with his subject." Throughout

1964

these stories a "sense of some perverse or capricious power"
is evident.

40 KEENAN, JOSEPH T. "Books." Extension 59 (June): 4.
      Review of The Wapshot Scandal. Finds fault with the
    novel's lack of plot and superficial characterization, call-
    ing it a "sweeping, disjointed work of literary impressionism."
    Argues that the novel fails to entertain the reader, which is
    "fiction's first purpose," and instead is replete with "inde-
    fensible coincidences and incongruities."

41 KIRSCH, ROBERT R. "Cheever Caught in Transit in New Wapshot
      Selection." Los Angeles Times, 5 February, Part IV, p. 6.
      Review of The Wapshot Scandal. Contends that this novel
    is fragmented, being really "three long stories, plaited
    loosely together" by an author who appears "weary, bored and
    confused." Though Cheever may be trying "to go beneath
    appearance to see . . . transcendental reality," he does not
    succeed here. The trouble may well be "that the exposure of
    the emptiness and rootlessness is not enough."

42 LAMOTT, KENNETH. "Ups and Downs of New Fiction." Show 4
      (February): 53-54.
      Review of The Wapshot Scandal. Although Cheever has a
    talent for mordant humor, there is not much of it here.
    This novel is an assault on the American Dream of suburban
    security and "often erupts into ferocious despair." As a
    satire, it is only a partial success at best.

43 [LEE, ALWYN.] "Ovid in Ossining." Time 83 (27 March): 66-70,
      72.
      Cover story that traces Cheever's life and career through
    the publication of The Wapshot Scandal. Describes him as a
    moralist who deals more with archetypes than characters and
    who gives suburbia "the dignity of classical theatre." Sug-
    gests that the structure of many of his "mature stories"
    comes from "skeletons in the family closet," although today
    Cheever is "at peace with the past." Includes nine excerpts
    from his writing that reveal Cheever's "long view." Re-
    printed: 1969.15.

44 McGOVERN, HUGH. "A Look at Spring Fiction." America 110
      (29 February): 289.
      Review of The Wapshot Scandal. Finds that like most con-
    temporary fiction, the novel "scores no points, passes no
    judgements, proposes no corrections or cures for the social
    and personal blights it portrays." Criticizes Cheever for
    just telling us how he sees modern America instead of explain-
    ing "what he thinks about his depressing vision."

45 MITCHELL, ADRIAN. "Haunted and Bewitched." <u>New York Times Book Review</u>, 18 October, p. 5.
    Review of <u>The Brigadier and the Golf Widow</u>. Contends that although Cheever probably has not "increased his word power since he wrote 'The Enormous Radio,'" this collection indicates that he is "still the quick-eyed, haunted entertainer." Despite his "flimsy" moral fable "Metamorphoses," most of these stories effectively hint at many of the fears that torment modern suburbia.

46 MUDRICK, MARVIN. "Man Alive." <u>Hudson Review</u> 17 (Spring): 115-16.
    Review of <u>The Wapshot Scandal</u>. Finds the novel typical of <u>New Yorker</u> fiction in the worst sense, with its "cocktail-party archness, the quaint surprises of circumstance, the tunnel-vision attention to routine details and sense-impressions, the quick-sketch going-away dabs at characterization, [and] the tittering ham-handed irony." Laments that Glenway Westcott recommended this novel, because he is one "who should know better."

47 NICHOLS, LEWIS. "A Visit with John Cheever." <u>New York Times Book Review</u>, 5 January, p. 28.
    Interview. Cheever comments on his writing regimen, daily life, and why he dislikes teaching. Discusses the inception and publishing history of the Wapshot novels and notes that he spent two months and made 150 pages of notes writing "The Swimmer."

48 NYREN, DOROTHY. Review of <u>The Brigadier and the Golf Widow</u>. <u>Library Journal</u> 89 (15 October): 3972.
    Finds that this collection includes "some of the best stories of one of our best writers." Praises Cheever's ability to take the elements of daily life and shape them "into a mythic entity."

49 OZICK, CYNTHIA. "America Aglow." <u>Commentary</u> 38 (July): 66-67.
    Review of <u>The Wapshot Scandal</u>. Finds that the chief character here is the twentieth century, in all its deterioration. For the first time Cheever confronts "America-in-the-main" in this novel, instead of treating it piecemeal. By his sentimental use of old St. Botolphs however, as the ideal of American society, Cheever's ironic view of contemporary life becomes little more than a hollow and self-deceptive parody. Reprinted: 1969.15.

50 _____. "Cheever's Yankee Heritage." <u>Antioch Review</u> 24 (Summer): 263-67.

1964

> Review of The Wapshot Scandal. Praises Cheever's "crystal
> and perfectionist dedication to the weight of the word"; yet
> finds his irony forced and contrived. Cheever's limitation as
> a writer is that he has not heeded Chekhov's dictum that "a
> style should always be colder than its material." Cheever has
> become discontented with contemporary America and so has
> created the nostalgic, artificial world of Yankee Wapshots
> that is essentially fraudulent, invented "out of sentiment
> and wholesale self-pity."

51 PEDEN, WILLIAM. The American Short Story. Boston: Houghton
    Mifflin, pp. 46–55, passim.
>   Surveys his collections through Some People, Places, and
> Things That Will Not Appear in My Next Novel and sees the
> latter as "a letdown, fatigued and written in an over-casual
> manner, although most of Cheever's stories tend to be "thor-
> oughly disciplined." Reprinted: 1969.15; 1975.3.

52 POORE, CHARLES. "A Romp Through the Wapshot Landscapes." New
    York Times, 7 January, p. 31.
>   Review of The Wapshot Scandal. Suggests that this is more
> a "'second helping'" than a sequel to The Wapshot Chronicle.
> Finds that the Wapshots cannot really marry people since "they
> are born married to their land, their traditions," and it is
> around such a premise that Cheever builds this "plot-loose
> and fancy soaring" novel. Notes also that because of the
> variety of Cheever's "inventions," one is never certain "what
> to consider the crucial Wapshot Scandal."

53 PRESCOTT, ORVILLE. "John Cheever's Comedy and Dismay." New York
    Times, 14 October, p. 43.
>   Review of The Brigadier and the Golf Widow. Views this
> collection as evidence that Cheever "is one of the most
> gifted, original and interesting" American writers today.
> Finds that Cheever tempers his satiric vision of America "with
> sympathy and pity." Praises him for "the wry humor, the
> bizarre imagination and the verbal grace" that inform this
> collection.

54 PRYCE-JONES, ALAN. "Banana Skins Where Angels Tread." New York
    Herald Tribune, 4 January, p. 7.
>   Review of The Wapshot Scandal. Sees this novel as a col-
> lection of "flashes of insight or wit," but lacking in "inner
> coherence." The many diverse elements are never pulled to-
> gether to form a novel, and instead, Cheever's self-indulgence
> results in a work "too capricious to be satisfying."

55 READ, DAVID W. "Cheever at His Best." St. Louis Post-Dispatch, 15 November, p. 4-B.
  Review of The Brigadier and the Golf Widow. Maintains that Cheever's "special talent" is his ability for "making much out of little" and finds that this collection is "an astonishing display of virtuosity." Notes that the range suggested by the stories "The Swimmer," "Metamorphoses," "The Music Teacher," and "The Seaside Houses" creates the impression that Cheever "is really Saki and Kafka and himself at once--a very neat trick and a very great treat."

56 RYAN, STEPHEN. Review of The Wapshot Scandal. Ave Maria 99 (7 March): 23.
  Finds this a powerful and important novel, written "with verve and style," in which Cheever's view of life "is perhaps slanted toward older values." Praises Cheever's perceptivity in analyzing suburban pretension and modern American life generally. In its attack on contemporary life's "sterility and materialism," this novel is "a little unnerving" and can be considered "a very moral book."

57 SAAL, ROLLENE W. "Pick of the Paperbacks." Saturday Review 47 (22 August): 34.
  Notes publication of The Housebreaker of Shady Hill.

58 _____. "Pick of the Paperbacks." Saturday Review 47 (26 December): 41.
  Describes The Housebreaker of Shady Hill as a collection of "stories, usually sad and suburban."

59 SALVESEN, CHRISTOPHER. "A Hieroglyph." New Statesman 68 (11 September): 366.
  Review of The Wapshot Scandal. Finds this novel "a crowded compendium of incident and fun." Argues that Cheever's discursive approach brings about an air of unreality, so that "everything is reduced to an aspect of the author's inventiveness."

60 SEGAL, DAVID. "Change Is Always for the Worse." Commonweal 81 (4 December): 362-63.
  Review of The Brigadier and the Golf Widow. Sees the theme of this collection to be "the chanciness of possessions." Cheever writes in a suave style about people who live like the rich while plagued by insecurity. He touches the horror beneath the surface of his characters' lives, but "it is horror recollected in detachment."

1964

61 SHABAD, THEODORE. "U.S. Writers Gain Russian Readers." New York
      Times, 27 October, p. 44.
        Reports that Cheever and John Updike, "whose names are
      virtually unknown here," are separately visiting the Soviet
      Union for a month each, where their work is now being
      translated.

62 SPENCER, DAVID G. Review of The Wapshot Scandal. The Critic 22
      (February–March): 74–75.
        Describes this as a remarkable and well-unified novel and
      considers Cheever a contemporary Matthew Arnold in his con-
      cern for the isolated individual in an irrational world.
      Coverly Wapshot emerges as "the Arnoldian character eternally
      searching for love," beaten yet invincible, with Honora repre-
      senting the failure of tradition, and Moses and Melissa the
      failure of marriage.

63 STRATFORD, PHILIP. "Spofford, Spofford and Sprockett."
      Saturday Night 79 (May): 28–39.
        Review of The Wapshot Scandal. Notes that Cheever's char-
      acterizations reveal that "human oddity intrigues him; eccen-
      tricity gives him confidence." Finds that the novel's title
      refers to "the scandal, the ridiculousness and the outrageous
      glory of being human."

64 SULLIVAN, RICHARD. "'Incomparable' Storyteller." Chicago
      Sunday Tribune, "Books Today," 25 October, p. 4.
        Review of The Brigadier and the Golf Widow. Contends that
      Cheever is a writer so unique as to obviate comparison with
      other writers. Describes him as "simultaneously both a very
      funny and a very sorrowful writer" and praises his ability to
      convey what is "grievously wrong with the world" without
      becoming didactic.

65 _____. "A Zany, Complex Work of Art That's a Delight to Read."
      Chicago Sunday Tribune, "Books Today," 12 January, p. 1.
        Review of The Wapshot Scandal. Finds the cumulative effect
      of the novel "like that of a narrative mosaic, with all the
      bits and pieces . . . combining together in unity." Praises
      Cheever's "governed and controlled prose," his lively and
      convincing characterizations, and his panoramic scope. The
      result is a "delightful, complex work of art in words."

66 WEALES, GERALD. "Wapshot in the Dark." The Reporter 30
      (16 January): 51–52.
        Review of The Wapshot Scandal. Unlike The Wapshot Chron-
      icle's celebration of life, this work is a novel about death
      and disintegration. Cheever's world has become lifeless, and

the virtues that once offered some consolation, including
Cheever's humor and understanding, are now gone.

67 WESCOTT, GLENWAY. "A Surpassing Sequel." New York Herald
    Tribune Book Week, 5 January, pp. 1, 9.
        Review of The Wapshot Scandal. Describes Cheever's
    writing as "somewhat too brilliant and sensuous" to be read
    casually. Finds his sentences "euphonious and emotional,"
    rather than "functional" or "emphatic," and sees Cheever's
    sense of proportion in maintaining its various "perspectives"
    as one of the "secrets of the unity" of this novel. Concludes
    that Cheever is an American existentialist in that the novel
    is more "visionary and reportorial" than "dramatic."

68 YARBROUGH, TOM. "The World of the Wapshots." St. Louis Post-
    Dispatch, 19 January, p. 4-C.
        Review of The Wapshot Scandal. Contends that this novel
    "marks a milestone of improvement since The Wapshot Chronicle"
    and praises Cheever for his development of "heavy themes with
    light touches." Since style is more important than content in
    this novel, the convoluted plot "is more than made up for by
    the author's gift of phrasing."

1965

1 ANON. "The Artless and the Arch." Times Literary Supplement
    64 (6 May): 356.
        Review of The Brigadier and the Golf Widow. Detects a
    mode of desperation in these stories that is "alarmingly
    rife." Finds Cheever mannered and stylized and imagines him
    writing with a smile that is "by turns world-wearied, tiger-
    ish and arch."

2 ANON. "New Short Stories." Times (London), 8 April, p. 15.
        Review of The Brigadier and the Golf Widow. Sees a
    "blend of roguishness and sentimentality" in a number of
    these stories and considers "The Ocean" among the best.

3 ANON. Review of The Brigadier and the Golf Widow. The Critic
    23 (February-March): 89.
        Finds these stories "well-polished, entertaining, non-
    psycho-straining." Describes Cheever's approach as "reportor-
    ial, though upon reflection it is artfully selective."

4 BROPHY, BRIGID. "Four Fours." New Statesman 69 (23 April):
    655.
        Review of The Brigadier and the Golf Widow. Contends that
    these stories tend to be surrealistic and peopled with

1965

characters who are "eccentric, halucinated, doomed or merely
in some ways <u>awful</u>." Finds Cheever's style "smooth, faintly
old-fashioned, literate and allusive."

5 COLEMAN, JOHN. "Exurban stresses." <u>Observer</u> (London), 28 March,
   p. 26.
      Review of <u>The Brigadier and the Golf Widow</u>. Considers
   these stories of exurbanites going "quietly out of their
   minds" closer—when "at their blackest"—to the work of
   Dorothy Parker or "Thurber in a bad mood" than to the crack-
   ups chronicled by Fitzgerald or Salinger. Praises Cheever for
   catching so "thriftily and well" the "accents and angsts" of
   his characters and finds that the least effective stories here,
   "Metamorphoses" and "The Angel of the Bridge," are such because "magic and myth are introduced."

6 Editors of <u>Time</u>. "Editors' Preface" to <u>The Wapshot Chronicle</u>.
   Time Reading Program Special Edition. New York: Time-Life,
   pp. ix-xv.
      Summarizes the novel and then argues that it is "a virtu-
   oso performance." Finds that Cheever's prose is both lyrical
   and economical. Though the novel is, on one level, "pure
   entertainment," it is "at bottom a serious novel and . . . an
   intensely moral one." It is also a "better book" than its
   sequel, <u>The Wapshot Scandal</u>.

7 ELLIOTT, GEORGE P. "Exploring the Province of the Short Story."
   <u>Harper's</u> 320 (April): 114.
      Review of <u>The Brigadier and the Golf Widow</u>. Finds this
   collection of mixed quality and notes that "The Swimmer" may
   be "pleasant enough" for the <u>New Yorker</u>, but it does not merit
   inclusion here. "Clementina" is the reviewer's favorite,
   because "her wonder is never frivolous as her author's often
   is," and the story itself is warm and not at all mocking.

8 GILROY, HARRY. "Cheever to Get Howells Medal for Writing
   Wapshot Scandal." <u>New York Times</u>, 24 March, p. 39.
      Reports that the award will be presented on May 19 and
   includes Cheever's comments on his six-week visit to the
   Soviet Union.

9 HART, JAMES D., ed. "John Cheever." <u>The Oxford Companion to
   American Literature</u>. New York: Oxford University Press,
   p. 149.
      Lists Cheever's work through 1964 and refers to his expul-
   sion from Thayer Academy as the point where his literary
   career began.

10 HEYEN, WILLIAM. Review of The Brigadier and the Golf Widow.
    Studies in Short Fiction 3 (Fall): 79–80.
         Includes Cheever among "our half-dozen most important
    living writers" and finds that these witty and charming
    stories have "a deceptive simplicity that at once entertains
    and edifies." Describes Cheever's vision as "sensitive,
    poetic," his language as "dazzling," and "his imagination
    vivid." Reprinted: 1975.4.

11 IGOE, W. J. Review of The Wapshot Scandal. The Month 33
    (February): 131–32.
         Describes Cheever's attitude toward life as "Victorian" and
    notes that he shares a nostalgic view of Italy with Hawthorne,
    James, and Melville. Finds that Cheever "is a Christian and
    consequently a comic writer" and that his tender treatment of
    his quirky characters "makes something like poetry of his
    comedy."

12 IPSEN, HENNING. "En mursten pa natbordet" [A Brick on the Night
    Table]. Zyllandsposten (Denmark), 23 September.
         Review of The Wapshot Chronicle. Finds this novel to be
    "executed with an ever present humor" and describes Cheever's
    irony as both "festive" and still quick to attack "hypocrisy
    and cant."

13 KAUFFMANN, STANLEY. "Literature of the Early Sixties: Cheever,
    Fitzgerald, Hemingway." Wilson Library Bulletin 39 (May):
    766–67.
         Comments generally on Cheever's career but focuses on The
    Wapshot Scandal. Finds this novel "at least as patchwork" as
    The Wapshot Chronicle, but in the sequel "this fault seems
    more important because the author's method is more discursive."
    Still, Cheever's humor and his finely polished prose "are
    stronger than ever."

14 LEVINE, NORMAN. "Places and People." Spectator 214 (23 April):
    538.
         Review of The Brigadier and the Golf Widow. Finds that
    Cheever is at his best when he makes fantasies out of his
    suburban material, as in "The Swimmer" or "The Angel of the
    Bridge." Some of his other stories, however, "tend to begin
    well and then disintegrate by being too cosy." The weakest
    stories here concern Americans abroad; while readable, they
    are "essentially light entertainment."

15 LITVINOVA, TATYANA. "John Cheever's The Brigadier and the Golf
    Widow." Questions of Literature (USSR), no. 2.

1965

> Describes Cheever as a "musical writer" and this collection
> as "a kind of musical suite." Finds that the theme of expa-
> triation "runs through the entire book like a cold wave," and
> its crest is in "A Woman Without a Country." Yet, considers
> "The Swimmer" the collection's most important story and con-
> cludes that Cheever's "muse helps the reader go fearlessly
> over the bridge built across the abyss of despair which John
> Cheever shows us so mercilessly." Reprinted: 1972.8.

16 MOHN, BENT. "Det gamle New England: Den menneskekaerlige
puritaner John Cheever og hans første roman" [Old New England:
That benevolent Puritan John Cheever and his first novel].
Politiken (Denmark), 4 September.
> Review of The Wapshot Chronicle. Sees Cheever's strength
> as his ability to create characters who are "strange yet
> credible," firmly fixed in a landscape that is delineated
> with a special sweetness, as if seen for the first--or the
> last--time. Cheever is "astonishingly old-fashioned, yet
> astonishingly new."

17 PETERSEN, CLARENCE. "Helping Hand for Caveat Emptor." Chicago
Sunday Tribune, "Books Today," 17 January, p. 9.
> Review of The Wapshot Scandal. Notes that this sequel
> "strikes more relevantly at the truths of today" than did
> The Wapshot Chronicle.

18 _____. "Personal Choices for Personal Pleasure." Chicago Sunday
Tribune, "Books Today," 28 February, p. 13.
> Review of The Wapshot Scandal. Notes that Cheever has
> "written this novel "with relevance, insight, and humor in a
> style of wry poetic imagery."

19 SCULLY, JAMES. "An Oracle of Subocracy." The Nation 200
(8 February): 144-45.
> Review of The Brigadier and the Golf Widow. Notes that the
> plot is secondary in Cheever's fiction and that he "is most
> characteristic when stepping out from it" to deliver a moral
> or to "relish with the reader some of the windfalls and pit-
> falls of storytelling." Throughout, this collection "seldom
> intimates passion or a vision."

20 SMALLWOOD, WILLIAM. Review of The Brigadier and the Golf Widow.
Extension 59 (March): 9-10.
> Although this collection is generally "superb," the last
> two stories "do not come off as well as" the rest, which is
> entertaining and well crafted. The last two pieces are "con-
> templative exercises in and out of focus."

21 STRAUMANN, HEINRICH. <u>American Literature in the Twentieth Century</u>. New York: Harper & Row, pp. 139-40.
     Finds that Cheever is mainly concerned with the "absurd" and that the structural principle behind his writing is "that of surprise through deluded expectation."

22 TREVOR, WILLIAM. "New Fiction." <u>The Listener</u> 73 (1 April): 497.
     Review of <u>The Brigadier and the Golf Widow</u>. Praises Cheever's "waspish, healthy vigour," which is evident through much of this collection, although at times Cheever leans toward "sententiousness." Notes that his style is crisp and "his dialogue never flags." While these stories "are admirably readable and informative," one is able to notice, in places, "the process of turning a wheeze into a story."

1966

1 ALDRIDGE, JOHN W. "John Cheever and the Soft Sell of Disaster." In <u>Time to Murder and Create: The Contemporary Novel in Crisis</u>, pp. 171-77. New York: David McKay.
     Reprint of 1964.1.

2 ANON. "L'allegro stacello di una famiglia USA" [The happy destruction of an American family]. <u>Gazetta Di Mantova</u> (Italy), 26 March.
     Review of <u>The Wapshot Scandal</u>. Sees the novel as "a blunt caricature" of certain modes of modern American life and thought. The narrative is midway between "ironic realism and a naturalistic dream," and the result is the creation of a disturbed and arbitrary reality.

3 ANON. "Ironia e realismo di Cheever" [Cheever's realism and irony]. <u>Paese Sera</u> (Italy), 13 May.
     Review of <u>The Wapshot Scandal</u>. Finds that with a mixture of realism and irony, Cheever evokes a nostalgic picture of the past. Notes that despite his popular success, Cheever's work has thus far received superficial critical attention.

4 ARVIDSSON, INGRID. "Vulkaner i medelaldern" [Volcanoes in middle age]. <u>Dagens Nyheter</u> (Sweden), 17 January, pp. 4-5.
     Discusses <u>The Wapshot Scandal</u> and <u>The Brigadier and the Golf Widow</u>. Finds that Cheever moves smoothly, ironically, and with a little melancholy through America's new world of bedroom communities, markets, airports, bomb shelters, and computers, finding human breakdown and defeat in the midst of near perfection and great welfare. Praises Cheever's vitality and maturity and notes that he skilfully shows how

1966

men and women suppress knowledge of the cracks that lead into
the molten heart of the volcano.

5 BRACHER, FREDERICK. "Sobremnnie mir, kaken ego bidet John
Cheever" [John Cheever's vision of modern life]. America
(USSR) 114 (Spring): 36–39.
Finds that more than other contemporary American writers,
John Cheever "is concerned about tradition and modernity, the
past and the present, and the relevance of both to the perilous business of living through the anxieties and uncertainties
of our time." Followed by an excerpt from The Wapshot Scandal
(pp. 39–42).

6 HYMAN, STANLEY EDGAR. "John Cheever's Golden Egg." In Standards:
A Chronicle of Books of Our Times, pp. 199–203. New York:
Horizon Press.
Reprint of 1964.36.

7 LID, R. W. "The Enormous Radio." In The Short Story: Classic
& Contemporary, pp. 43–44, 55–56. Philadelphia: J. B.
Lippincott.
Reprints the story with an introduction that contends that
Cheever's fiction is characterized by its "urbanity and rea-
sonableness." Describes Cheever as "more concerned with the
shortcomings and limitations of a class than with individuals"
and sees his characters as "typical and representative." Five
questions for discussion follow the story.

8 PASINETTI, P. M. "Lo scandalo Wapshot: Il libro piu letto in
America" [The Wapshot Scandal: The book most read in America].
Corriere della Sera (Italy), 14 June.
Sees Cheever as a "modern classical writer" in the tradition of James Gould Cozzens. Notes that despite the beauty
of the American landscape, Cheever's fictive world is "gray
and threadbare." He seems to consider his unhappy and materialistic characters as originals, while they are clichés and
even quite similar to many of Cheever's American readers.

9 PEDEN, WILLIAM. Introduction to Stories, by Jean Stafford, John
Cheever, Daniel Fuchs, and William Maxwell, pp. v–viii. New
York: Noonday Press.
Finds that among these fifteen stories, Peden's favorite is
Cheever's "The Day the Pig Fell into the Well." Explains that
"few if any short story writers have more successfully evoked
the spirit and mood of an earlier, more leisurely way of life
than Cheever has in this Indian-summer portrait of the Nudd
family." Praises Cheever's ability to "manipulate" his characters so adroitly.

<u>1967</u>

1 ANON. Review of <u>The Wapshot Scandal</u>. <u>Basil Nachrichten</u>
   (Germany), 7 October.
      Describes the novel as entertaining, although it seems that
   Cheever believes that a story without sex rarely succeeds.
   Finds that the novel is generally like "theatrical thunder"
   and not to be taken too seriously.

2 ANON. "Die Wapshots und andere" [The Wapshots and others].
   <u>Main-Echo</u> (Germany), 25 October.
      Review of <u>The Wapshot Scandal</u>. Sees Cheever as an excellent
   writer, who holds a mirror before the American people in this
   novel. The result is a realistic work that derives its charm
   from his anecdotal approach.

3 AUSER, CORTLAND P. "John Cheever's Myth of Man and Time: 'The
   Swimmer.'" <u>The CEA Critic</u> 29 (March): 18-19.
      Sees "The Swimmer" as Cheever's modern myth, in which he
   uses the "themes of quest, journey, initiation and discovery"
   to comment on contemporary life. Describes Neddy Merrill's
   transformation as an Ovidian metamorphosis.

4 GOLD, HERBERT and STEVENSON, DAVID L., eds. "Editors'
   Analysis." In <u>Stories of Modern America</u>, p. 193. New York:
   St. Martin's Press.
      Reprint of 1961.17.

5 KENDLE, BURTON. "Cheever's Use of Mythology in 'The Enormous
   Radio.'" <u>Studies in Short Fiction</u> 4 (Spring): 262-64.
      Finds this story to be "an ironic reinterpretation of the
   Eden story" and sees the radio as the "Satanic invader" of
   the couple's innocent world.

<u>1968</u>

1 ANON. "Paperbacks." <u>Times</u> (London), 29 June, p. 25.
      Review of <u>The Wapshot Scandal</u>. Describes the novel as
   "strangely unshaped," although it does have its "moments of
   high comic criticism."

2 KAZIN, ALFRED. "Our Middle-Class Storytellers." <u>Atlantic
   Monthly</u> 222 (August): 51-55.
      Mentioning Cheever's work throughout, he finds "The Death
   of Justina" a "marvelously witty social commentary," while
   attributing the success of "The Country Husband" more to
   Cheever's style than to his characterizations.

1969

1 ANON. Review of <u>Bullet Park</u>. <u>Booklist</u> 65 (15 May): 1060.
      Notes that the novel "superbly" illuminates many contempo-
   rary issues.

2 ANON. Review of <u>Bullet Park</u>. <u>Choice</u> 6 (July–August): 642.
      Finds that the novel does not match Cheever's Wapshot saga
   or <u>The Brigadier and the Golf Widow</u>, even though he "knows
   his American eccentrics and knows writing." This novel is
   "as schizophrenic as his characters" and its "structure is
   unsound."

3 ANON. "Books." <u>Playboy</u> 16 (April): 40.
      Review of <u>Bullet Park</u>. Finds that despite his originality
   and insight, this novel is "an ambitious disappointment."
   Contends that Cheever has stayed with his suburban settings
   too long and consequently has lost some of his characteristic
   "abrasive sense of graceful nonsense."

4 ANON. "Notes on Current Books." <u>Virginia Quarterly Review</u> 45
   (Autumn), cxxviii.
      Review of <u>Bullet Park</u>. Praises Cheever's sardonic humor
   and "his incomparable sense of pure irony." Despite the mo-
   notony of the protagonists' lives he is describing, Cheever
   remains a consistently interesting craftsman throughout the
   novel.

5 ANON. "The Portable Abyss." <u>Time</u> 93 (25 April): 109.
      Review of <u>Bullet Park</u>. Suggests that here, as in his
   earlier work, Cheever is "something of a Christian soldier in
   mufti, a man more kin to John Bunyan than to John Updike."
   However, this novel is also a departure for Cheever, "a
   thrusting out from rational story telling to the presentation
   of linked fragments of life." As such, the novel is "crude,
   yet mysteriously provocative."

6 ANON. "16 Western Intellectuals Score Soviet Attacks on
   Solzhenitsyn." <u>New York Times</u>, 5 December, p. 47.
      Mentions Cheever as a signatory of a letter sent to Moscow
   condemning the expulsion of Solzhenitsyn from the Soviet
   writers' union.

7 ANON. "Subtopian Sicknesses." <u>Times Literary Supplement</u> 68
   (30 October): 1249.
      Review of <u>Bullet Park</u>. Finds that while the novel is a
   "remarkably convincing fantasy," it presents not two halves
   of the American psyche, as the dust jacket proclaims, but

only "two types of sad suburbanite." Praises Cheever's delicacy and "persuasive conviction" with which he treats "the great public issues that lead to private grief."

8 BELL, PEARL K. "Taker of Notes." The New Leader 52 (26 May): 11-13.
   Review of Bullet Park. Argues that "there is something strangely misguided and botched, fundamentally wrongheaded" about this novel. Finds Cheever's purpose "fatally vague" and unfocused, and though the novel opens well enough, it ends "in a violent parody of murder and salvation." The various episodes seem like little more than "rough notes for a short story."

9 BORG, MARY. "Yarn." New Statesman 78 (12 September): 347-48.
   Review of Bullet Park. Finds that when the novel moves into the world of fantasy, "things begin to fall apart." Contends that Cheever is "more interested in effect than truth" and puts great emphasis on his "skilled, detached, sometimes prolix" style.

10 BROYARD, ANATOLE. "You Wouldn't Believe It." New Republic 160 (26 April): 36-37.
   Review of Bullet Park. Finds that Cheever "appears to be almost helplessly carried away by the flood tides of his imagination" in this "Gothic" novel. Describes the plot as improbable and notes that "Cheever's palette seems to have nothing but screaming colors." The result is something of an amoral morality play that Cheever "determined to be surprising or original, even at the cost of incredulity."

11 BURHANS, CLINTON S., JR. "John Cheever and the Grave of Social Coherence." Twentieth Century Literature 14 (January): 187-98.
   Argues that Cheever is not merely a "whimsical New Yorker satirist," but rather a "major chronicler of contemporary absurdity" and "a trenchant moralist." In addition, since the mid-1950s his fiction, especially the Wapshot novels and The Brigadier and the Golf Widow, has been concerned with the fact that, as Cheever put it, "'something has gone very wrong.'" The major catastrophes that his characters face occur when there is a disturbance within their social order. That these disruptions are becoming a contemporary commonplace "appalls Cheever," and it is this concern that "suggests a thoroughly contemporary and potentially major tragic vision of man." Reprinted: 1973.32.

1969

12 COLLIER, PETER. "Fable for Our Time." The Progressive 33
       (July): 33-34.
         Review of Bullet Park. Sees this novel as a "peculiarly
       modern" allegory, laden with portentous symbolism. However,
       the ending is weak and inadequate and leaves too many ques-
       tions unanswered.

13 CORBETT, EDWARD P. J. Review of Bullet Park. America 120
       (24 May): 630-32.
         Finds this "novella" indicative of "the same economical
       craftsmanship" that Cheever demonstrates in his short stories.
       Though the reviewer supposes that Cheever is making an allegor-
       ical statement, he confesses that he is "out of his depth" to
       interpret it. Concludes that the novel tugs at "one's arche-
       typal memories."

14 CURLEY, DOROTHY. Review of Bullet Park. Library Journal 94
       (15 February), 777-78.
         Contends that Cheever is "at his best" here because he has
       effectively integrated his motifs into one story. His detail
       of suburban malaises is "masterful."

15 CURLEY, DOROTHY NYREN; KRAMER, MAURICE; and KRAMER, ELAINE
       FIALKA, eds. "John Cheever." In A Library of Literary
       Criticism: Modern American Literature. 4th ed., pp. 211-16.
       New York: Frederick Ungar.
         Reprints excerpts of: 1943.3; 1943.6; 1943.7; 1953.14;
       1957.8; 1957.14; 1957.15; 1958.7; 1958.8; 1964.21; 1964.43;
       1964.49; 1964.51.

16 DAVENPORT, GUY. "Elegant Botches." National Review 21 (3 June):
       549-50.
         Review of Bullet Park. Argues that Cheever has taken the
       plot of Beckett's Molloy and transposed it to a suburban
       setting and used the surnames conceit of Endgame. The novel
       proceeds well enough and conveys a picture of suburban life
       that "makes one's soul ache." Yet, unlike Beckett, Cheever
       makes "no sense at all" at the end of the novel, which is
       "false and shockingly inept." After page 200, the story
       ceases to move forward and simply "comes to pieces," degener-
       ating into "pure hokum."

17 DeMOTT, BENJAMIN. "A Grand Gatherum [sic] of Some Late 20th-
       Century American Weirdos." New York Times Book Review,
       27 April, pp. 1, 40-41.
         Review of Bullet Park. Describes this novel as being less
       than first-rate, because it consists of "parts tacked together"
       flimsily and of characters drawn inconsistently. In addition,

Cheever ignores the demand for explanation inherent in the
novel-form and instead, writes Bullet Park in the style of a
short story. The result is a confusing novel, marked by
"carelessness, lax composition, [and] perfunctoriness."

18 DONALDSON, SCOTT. The Suburban Myth. New York: Columbia
    University Press, pp. 203-8, 248.
        Finds that like Phyllis McGinley, Cheever refuses to be a
    detractor of suburbia; yet he avoids being its defender.
    Notes that throughout his fiction Cheever evenhandedly recog-
    nizes both the problems and advantages of the suburbs, making
    clear that although life is ruined in suburbia, it is also
    equally flawed elsewhere by "the bitch goddess of success . . .
    [which] extends far beyond the borders of Remsen Park." In-
    cludes a selective survey of the critical assessment of
    Cheever's work from 1957 to 1969.

19 ELLMAN, MARY. "Recent Novels: The Languages of Art." Yale
    Review 59 (Autumn): 111-12.
        Review of Bullet Park. Argues that despite the cleverness
    of the novel, there is "a dismaying solipsism" about it: the
    world of Bullet Park "is a world within a book within the same
    world." The result is that in the end we learn from this novel
    what we already knew, and Cheever's world of good and evil be-
    comes banal, with "the easy availability of trials, tempta-
    tions, and salvations."

20 FULLER, EDMUND. "Uneven Cheever." Wall Street Journal,
    29 April, p. 20.
        Review of Bullet Park. Finds that some parts of the novel
    are better than the whole because of its episodic, uneven
    construction. Still, it is "erratically brilliant" and a
    "swirling blend of the funny, the grotesque, the terrible
    and the shrewd realistic observation."

21 GRANT, ANNETTE. "The Hammer and the Nail." Newsweek 73
    (28 April): 101-03, 106.
        Review of Bullet Park. Sees this novel as a "spare,
    architectural book centered upon the question of identity."
    Finds that the "curves and dalliances" of the Wapshot novels
    are not present here, but instead, Bullet Park is a coolly
    precise and religiously symbolic tale. Review also includes
    a brief biography and comments Cheever has made on his fic-
    tion, which he compares to "marriage or a long affair."

22 GRANT, LOUIS. "America's Nomads." Ramparts 8 (September):
    62, 64, 66.

1969

Review of <u>Bullet Park</u>. Describes this novel as a symbolic work in the manner of Nabokov, "pasted onto a very good contemporary problem play <u>a la</u> Playhouse 90." Defines the struggle between Hammer and Nailles as the "embodiment of the struggle between appearance and reality." Comments also on Cheever's career, contends that <u>The Wapshot Chronicle</u> may be compared to Faulkner's <u>Sartoris</u>, and terms Cheever "almost a Yankee Faulkner." Concludes that Cheever has not developed the mine of mythic possibilities of St. Botolphs as Faulkner did with his Jefferson.

23 GREENE, GEORGE. "The Road Through Nightmare." <u>Kenyon Review</u> 31, no. 4: 564-70.
Review of <u>Bullet Park</u>. Calls Cheever "the most underrated man of our American literary scene." Finds that despite the differences in character and setting, Eliot Nailles is a psychological descendant of Leander Wapshot, since the former "refuses to lapse into dementia by howling that he has lost control or that society, in any meaningful way, has ceased to exist."

24 HARTE, BARBARA and RILEY, CAROLYN, eds. "John Cheever." In <u>Contemporary Authors</u>. Vols. 5-8, pp. 210-12. Detroit: Gale Research Company.
Biographical essay that includes a survey of Cheever's critical reception. Provides brief primary and secondary bibliographies.

25 HICKS, GRANVILLE. "Literary Horizons." <u>Saturday Review</u> 52 (26 April): 32.
Review of <u>Bullet Park</u>. Finds that Cheever is not so much concerned with suburban life as he is with the "unpredictable, sometimes terrifying, but often good fun" of life itself. <u>Bullet Park</u> is not a well constructed novel, but unlike the episodic Wapshot novels, it does have a formal design.

26 HOOD, STUART. "Silver-Age Fun." <u>The Listener</u> 82 (18 September): 385.
Review of <u>Bullet Park</u>. Finds Cheever's style "ironical, self-parodying" and views the novel, in its depiction of small town life in America, as "both highly comic and very sad."

27 JACKSON, KATHERINE GAUSS. "Books in Brief." <u>Harper's</u> 238 (May): 102-3.
Review of <u>Bullet Park</u>. Describes the novel as an unconvincing and unmoving nightmare about suburbia. Although there were occasionally brilliantly written passages, the novel as a whole failed to make one care about the characters.

28 KAZIN, ALFRED. "The Alone Generation." In The American Novel
    Since World War II, edited by Marcus Klein, pp. 121-22.
    New York: Fawcett Publications.
        Reprint of 1962.2

29 KIRSCH, ROBERT. "Cheever Subtly Lights Up Bullet Park From
    Inside." Los Angeles Times, 20 April, pp. 38, 40.
        Review of Bullet Park. Contends that Cheever is "a master
    illusionist," who subtly and credibly reveals his main char-
    acters, showing that "neither man is what he appears to be."
    However, the author's reliance on madness at the end of the
    novel is "too easy a solution" for the complexities Cheever
    has presented. Finds that this "brilliant" exposé may well
    have resulted in a "masterpiece" had Cheever been willing to
    offer a solution for the malady he exposed.

30 LEHMANN-HAUPT, CHRISTOPHER. "Talk With John Cheever." New York
    Times Book Review, 27 April, pp. 42-44.
        Interview. Cheever comments on the experience of writing
    Bullet Park and notes that he does not intend to "work in that
    line again." He also discusses his future writing plans.

31 LEONARD, JOHN. "Evil Comes to Suburbia." New York Times,
    29 April, p. 43.
        Review of Bullet Park. Suggests that Hammer is intention-
    ally drawn as an unbelievable character, who may really be "an
    aspect or fantasy" that Nailles imagines to defeat and thereby
    redeem himself. Finds this novel "Cheever's deepest, most
    challenging book," having "the tension and luminosity of a
    vision."

32 MORSE, J. MITCHELL. "Brand Names and Others." The Hudson
    Review 22 (Summer): 323-26.
        Review of Bullet Park. Finds fault with Cheever's vocab-
    ulary (and English usage in general) and observes that
    "Cheever has always been an uneven writer, and he doesn't
    progress." Still, finds this novel "worth reading for its
    serious intent and its frequent intervals of good execution"
    and especially for the deft characterization of Paul Hammer.

33 MURRAY, MICHELE. "Tenderness in Cheever's Bullet Park."
    National Catholic Reporter 5 (30 April): 9.
        Review of Bullet Park. Finds that Cheever's "most remark-
    able quality" is the tenderness with which he reveals the
    banality of life in Bullet Park, while continuing to care for
    his characters. This memorable book is akin to Percy's The
    Moviegoer "in its complexity, theme, [and] humor."

1969

34 NICOL, CHARLES. "Salvation in the Suburbs." <u>Atlantic Monthly</u>
223 (May): 96, 98.
Review of <u>Bullet Park</u>. Finds that this novel has a "clean
plot line," and unlike the Wapshot novels, it does not digress.
Still, <u>Bullet Park</u> is disappointing because of an unconvincing
plot "that weakens toward the end." Furthermore, much could
have been made of the view through the eyes of the idiot
Hammer, as Faulkner did in <u>The Sound and the Fury</u>.

35 NORDELL, RODERICK. "Cheever's Suburbs of the Heart." <u>Christian
Science Monitor</u>, 1 May, p. B-10.
Review of <u>Bullet Park</u>. Suggests that it "does not pay to
puzzle at" the diverting symbols and allegory of this
narrative.

36 OATES, JOYCE CAROL. "Cheever's People: The Retreat from Chaos."
<u>Chicago Tribune Book World</u>, 20 April, pp. 1, 3.
Review of <u>Bullet Park</u>. Contends that "Cheever's talky,
fragmented, at times exasperating method of narration" reflects the general predicament of his characters: "how to
remain sane?" <u>Bullet Park</u> itself is more "a series of eerie,
sometimes beautiful, sometimes overwrought vignettes," than a
novel, and Cheever's pervasive irony tends to obscure the
point "where whimsy begins and a real nastiness, a profound
nastiness, begins."

37 O'MALLEY, MICHAEL. "Do-It-Yourself Crucifixions." <u>The Critic</u>
27 (June-July): 78-80.
Review of <u>Bullet Park</u>. Considers <u>The Wapshot Chronicle</u>
Cheever's best novel, but finds <u>Bullet Park</u> better than <u>The
Wapshot Scandal</u>. Contends that <u>Bullet Park</u> is flawed by
being too diffuse and by having no character "large enough
for real tragedy. Nailles has no guts; Hammer's are all
turned into paranoid bitterness."

38 PETERSEN, CLARENCE. "Mixed company." <u>Chicago Tribune Book
World</u>, 5 October, p. 17.
Review of <u>The Housebreaker of Shady Hill</u>. Notes that each
story "exhibits the wit, control and paradoxical talent for
bizarre understatement" that are characteristic of Cheever's
fiction.

39 RATCLIFFE, MICHAEL. "The Great American Unease." <u>Times</u> (London),
13 September, p. 4.
Review of <u>Bullet Park</u>. Explains that while Cheever is
among the "finest storytellers writing in English today," he
does not achieve the coherence of his Wapshot novels in
<u>Bullet Park</u>. This novel would have been more effective as

a novella. Cheever's use of separate, complimentary sections for Hammer and Nailles "seems contrived," and the result is "just a little too pat."

40 SCHLUETER, PAUL. "Radical Departure." Christian Century 86 (21 May): 715.
   Review of Bullet Park. Considers this departure from Cheever's earlier satires and social commentaries as an "embarrasing reminder of what Cheever can do and has done in the past." Although the style of this novel is polished, the characterization and plot are so carelessly handled that if Cheever were not such a well-known writer, this novel "would probably never have been published."

41 SHAPIRO, CHARLES. "This Familiar and Lifeless Scene." Nation 208 (30 June): 836-37.
   Review of Bullet Park. Finds the episodic quality of this novel an effective way of communicating the isolated lives "of friends and enemies" and their "attempt to make connections." Notes also that the novel has a number of mythic and biblical analogues and that Nailles' anguish "is worthy of our attention and concern." The happy ending indicates that Cheever has gone "beyond satire to truth"; "there are no cheap giggles in this beautiful book."

42 SHAW, RUSSELL. Review of Bullet Park. The Sign 48 (June): 55-56.
   Views this novel as a parable, though a disappointing one, since at the end the "promising metaphor . . . fails somehow to come off successfully." The meaning of the confrontation between Hammer and Nailles is never explained and is "perhaps inexplicable." Since Cheever refuses to provide an answer to his "puzzle," Bullet Park is ultimately an "unsettling," if "often brilliant" novel.

43 SHEED, WILFRED. "Critics' Choices for Christmas." Commonweal 91 (5 December): 319.
   The reviewer admits that Cheever "is my favorite American stylist" and recommends The Enormous Radio and The Brigadier and the Golf Widow.

44 _____. "Mr. Saturday, Mr. Monday and Mr. Cheever." Life 66 (18 April): 39-40, 44, 46.
   Profile of Cheever, which describes him as "our subtlest and most sympathetic interpreter" of suburban paranoia. Includes biographical sketch, mentions Bullet Park, and quotes Cheever's comparison of novels to movies as being what a bell is to a whistle: "No resonance."

1969

45 SLOAT, WARREN. Review of <u>Bullet Park</u>. <u>Commonweal</u> 90 (9 May):
       241–42.
          Suggests that Cheever "unconvincingly tries to validate
       bourgeois life" throughout this novel. Since Hammer's destruc-
       tive plans are neutralized at the end of the novel, it seems
       that Cheever is not writing creative fiction, but rather ex-
       pressing "the editorial policy of our responsible journals."

46 TUBE, HENRY. "Verification." <u>Spectator</u> 223 (20 September): 375.
          Review of <u>Bullet Park</u>. Praises Cheever for breathing new
       life into seemingly trite material and calls this novel "a
       kind of a Diary of a Madman set inside a Diary of a Nobody."

47 UPDIKE, JOHN. "Suburban men." <u>Sunday Times</u> (London),
       14 September, p. 62.
          Review of <u>Bullet Park</u>. Finds that this novel "holds to-
       gether but just barely, by the thinnest of threads." Contends
       that the novel succeeds "as a slowly revolving mobile of mar-
       vellously poeticized moments" and that Cheever is now speaking
       "increasingly in the accents of a visionary." Reprinted:
       1975.5; 1977.60.

48 VINCE, THOMAS L. Review of <u>Bullet Park</u>. <u>Best Sellers</u> 29
       (15 May): 63–64.
          Finds that Cheever, in this "biting and brilliant" novel,
       is concerned with "the seeming lack of purpose that makes
       even 'the good life' appear pointless." Although the novel
       may seem to be little more than a series of loosely unified
       episodes, it is still "splendid" as an excursion into the
       heart of "a terrible kind of darkness."

49 WOLFE, PETER. "Mr. Cheever Again, in a Variety of Voices."
       <u>St. Louis Post-Dispatch</u>, 25 May, p. 4-C.
          Review of <u>Bullet Park</u>. Contends that this novel "is one
       of the most moving" novels of 1969 and praises the "variety
       of voices and methods" Cheever uses in telling his story.
       However, "nearly everything goes wrong" in the last seven
       chapters: his "narrative focus blurs, his story-line loses
       its cutting edge, the thread running through his incidents
       gets lost." Thus, despite the craftsmanship evident in much
       of the novel, the effect of the entire work is "baffling and
       bewitching," and <u>Bullet Park</u> is "the literary enigma of the
       season."

<u>1970</u>

1 ANON. "Il dramma quasi religioso dei nostri valori in crisi"
       [A quasi-religious drama of the crisis of our values].
       <u>La Tribune Politica</u> (Rome), 3 July.

Review of <u>Bullet Park</u>. Describes this novel as being mid-
way between "ironic realism and naturalistic dream" and compares Cheever to Hawthorne in his technique of presenting a
narrative through multiple points of view.

2 ANON. "Paperbacks." <u>Publishers Weekly</u> 197 (9 March): 89.
  Notice of paperback publication of <u>Bullet Park</u>, <u>The Wapshot
  Chronicle</u>, <u>The Wapshot Scandal</u>, and <u>The Brigadier and the Golf
  Widow</u>.

3 CREMASCHI, INISERO. "Malabolgia americana" [The American
  confusion]. <u>L'Avvenire</u> (Italy), 24 July.
    Review of <u>Bullet Park</u>. Finds that Cheever does not make
  any judgments on his characters but simply exposes the reality
  of a neurotic modern society.

4 G., E. "Un silenzio piu eloquente della parola" [A more eloquent
  silence of the word]. <u>Gionale Di Bergamo</u> (Italy), 23 July.
    Review of <u>Bullet Park</u>. Finds that here Cheever realisti-
  cally depicts the American "silent majority," trapped by their
  own efficient system. Notes also that despite his similarity
  to the <u>New Yorker</u> writers, Cheever differs in his ironic touch
  and in his warm understanding of human nature.

5 KAMPMANN, CHRISTIAN. Review of <u>Bullet Park</u>. <u>Information</u>
  (Denmark), 18 June.
    Finds that the American novel seems committed to the
  WASPishness of suburbia. In this arena, Cheever is reserved,
  witty, ironic, urbane, accessible, and not given to allegory.
  We may rejoice that he is no Lagerkvist.

6 MENDELSON, MORIS O. "Social Criticism in the Works of Bellow,
  Updike, and Cheever." In <u>Problems of Twentieth Century American Literature</u>, edited by Morris O. Mendelson, A. N.
  Nikolyukin, and R. M. Samarin. Moscow.
    Finds that although some of Cheever's work is often
  "diverting," other of his work is "profoundly satirical."
  In this latter category "one perceives an acknowledgement
  of the amorality of capitalistic higher circles in the United
  States, and still he has given in to the influence of circles
  which pursue aims hostile to socialism." Reprinted: 1972.8.

7 MOHN, BENT. "Forstadsborger i USA" [Suburbanite in the U.S.A.].
  <u>Politiken</u> (Denmark), 23 May, p. 10.
    Review of <u>Bullet Park</u>. Notes that although Cheever is a
  "lovely teller of tales," this is the weakest of his three
  novels. He is better with his short stories, the best now
  written in America. If his Danish publisher really wants to
  pamper us, he should give us a selection right away.

1970

8 MULYARCHEK, A. "O novom romane Dzhona Chivera" [About a new
   novel by John Cheever]. <u>Inostrannaia Literatura</u> (Moscow) 8:
   158-61.
       Review of <u>Bullet Park</u>. Briefly discusses the Wapshot
   novels but considers <u>Bullet Park</u> Cheever's "most mature work"
   and even the most important event in American literature in
   1969. Finds that in this novel Cheever is more precise than
   he has been before, and through grim satire he reveals the
   spiritual poverty in America. Since he depicts how boring,
   sinister, and at times even insane life is in contemporary
   America, his novel is controversial, but nevertheless, it is
   honest.

9 P., P. "Tragedia segreta" [Secret tragedy]. <u>Il Secolo</u> (Italy),
   27 June.
       Review of <u>Bullet Park</u>. Finds that Cheever does not succeed
   in giving a universal meaning to the crisis of values he
   dramatizes.

10 PETERSEN, CLARENCE. "Paperbacks." <u>Chicago Tribune Book World</u>,
   10 May, p. 17.
       Notes paperback publication of <u>Bullet Park</u>.

11 RUPP, RICHARD H. "John Cheever: The Upshot of Wapshot." In
   <u>Celebration in Postwar American Fiction, 1945-1967</u>, pp. 27-39,
   passim. Coral Gables, Fla.: University of Miami Press.
       Focuses on the Wapshot novels and contends that their
   "abiding quality" is not in plot but in "a ceremonial style:
   the significant action, as exuberant and vital as it is,
   works itself out in formal, ritualized gestures." Sees the
   ceremonies in <u>The Wapshot Scandal</u> as "less nostalgic and more
   relevant" than those of its predecessor and contends that the
   development of Cheever's style "reflects the essential need
   of contemporary life, the need for appropriate forms."
   Reprinted: 1976.9.

1971

1 CHESNICK, EUGENE. "The Domesticated Stroke of John Cheever."
   <u>New England Quarterly</u> 44 (December): 531-52.
       Considers Cheever a talented writer "who is struggling to
   make his fictional meanings in an increasingly frantic world"
   and surveys his work through <u>Bullet Park</u>. Contends that
   Cheever is working within the Transcendentalist tradition of
   Emerson and Thoreau and that Cheever has chosen Leander
   Wapshot to transmit "the principles of New England individualism." Leander is an heir to Thoreau, as the latter was an
   heir to Jonathan Edwards. In addition, as late as <u>Bullet Park</u>

Cheever, like Emerson, refuses to accept "the finality of evil." Ultimately, while the achievement of Cheever's career is still "inconclusive," it is clear that a "drastic change in the nature of individualism" has occurred. Reprinted: 1977.60.

2 GARDNER, JOHN. "Witchcraft in Bullet Park." New York Times Book Review, 24 October, pp. 2, 24.
    Review of Bullet Park. Describes this novel as a "magnificent work of fiction," while the Wapshot novels are "minor" works. Contends that most reviewers of Bullet Park were offended by Cheever's intimation that good and evil are merely the effects of chance. Finds also that the poetic devices "rhythm, imagistic repetition, [and] echo" and their "magical" implications are central to the novel's "ambiguous meaning." Reprinted: 1976.9.

3 GARRETT, GEORGE. "Afterword: John Cheever and the Charms of Innocence." In The Sounder Few: Essays from the "Hollins Critic," edited by R. H. W. Dillard, George Garrett, and John Rees Moore, pp. 33-41. Athens: University of Georgia Press.
    Assesses Cheever's two books since The Wapshot Scandal and finds that The Brigadier and the Golf Widow reveals "a new sense of technical innovation, an ease and playfulness . . . and more compassion." Sees this collection as also indicative of the development of "a sense of charity" evident in The Wapshot Scandal. However, in Bullet Park Cheever "is increasingly a cartoonist." This novel seems to be a scornful and self-righteous distortion of the world, having a "'happy ending'" that is negative and sarcastic. Includes biographical note and a primary bibliography through 1970. Reprint of 1964.27.

4 G[OLDMAN], A[RNOLD]. "John Cheever." In The Penguin Companion to Literature: U.S.A., edited by Eric Mottram and Malcolm Bradbury, p. 56. London: Penguin Press.
    Biographical essay. Notes that Cheever's tone is a mixture of nostalgia and satire and that his more recent work evinces "connections with the work of William Burroughs and Terry Southern."

5 GREENE, BEATRICE. "Icarus at St. Botolphs: A Descent to 'Unwonted Otherness.'" Style 5: 119-37.
    Sees the Wapshot novels as dominated by a motif of descent, by which Cheever traces the decline of the Wapshot family. This motif is underscored by his infusing these novels "with the disbalance and dis-equation that sends the reader falling."

1971

6 RAYMONT, HENRY. "Book Unit Rejects 'Love Story.'" New York
   Times, 22 January, p. 16.
      Reports that the National Book Committee panel of five
   fiction judges, of which Cheever is a member, threatened to
   resign if Erich Segal's Love Story is a candidate for a
   National Book Award.

7 R[ICHARDSON, K[ENNETH] R[IDLEY]. "John Cheever." In Twentieth
   Century Writing: A Reader's Guide to Contemporary Literature,
   edited by Kenneth Richardson and R. Clive Willis, p. 124.
   New York: Transatlantic Arts.
      Biographical note. Mentions Cheever's work through The
   Wapshot Scandal.

8 STENGEL, WAYNE BRENNAN. "Hammer and Nailles: The Problem of
   'Good' and 'Evil' in Bullet Park and Six Short Stories of
   John Cheever." Master's thesis, University of Louisville
   (Kentucky), 114 pp.
      Contends that "the Hammer-Nailles theme of two men at war
   with one another," one evil, one good, is the "dominant, recurrent" theme in Cheever's fiction. Traces this through
   Bullet Park and "The Summer Farmer," "Goodbye, My Brother,"
   "The Housebreaker of Shady Hill," "Brimmer," "The Angel of
   the Bridge," and "The Seaside Houses." Concludes that the
   novel and six stories also share the theme of "the loneliness
   of obsolescence," in that the various protagonists are all
   isolated by their obsession with their anachronistic concep-
   tion of "good" and "evil."

9 VANCURA, ZDENEK. "Soucasni americti romanopisci [Contemporary
   American novelists]: John Cheever." Časopis pro Moderní
   Filogii (Czechoslovakia), 53: 1-3.
      Finds the principal difference between the Wapshot novels
   to be Cheever's treatment of small town life. In the first
   novel he humorously portrays an old-fashioned village, whereas
   in the second novel he focuses on the negative effects of
   modernization of that rural world. In Bullet Park Cheever
   combines elements from his first two novels to reveal that
   the effect of this mixture is madness and crime. This third
   novel, then, is reminiscent of Truman Capote's In Cold Blood.

1972

1 ALDRIDGE, JOHN W. "John Cheever and the Soft Sell of Disaster."
   In The Devil in the Fire: Retrospective Essays of American
   Literature and Culture, 1951-1971, pp. 235-40. New York:
   Harper's Magazine Press.
      Reprint of 1964.1.

2 ANON. "Fiction in paperback." Times (London), 30 March, p. 12.
      Review of Bullet Park. Finds this novel "more contrived"
   than the Wapshot sagas, although this "tribal morality tale"
   is "diabolically well told."

3 CORKE, HILARY. "The Wapshot Scandal." In The Critic as Artist,
      edited by Gilbert A. Harrison, pp. 71-76. New York:
      Liveright.
         Reprint of 1964.18

4 EISINGER, CHESTER E. "John Cheever." In Contemporary Novelists,
      edited by James Vinson, pp. 251-53. New York: St. Martin's
      Press.
         Assesses Cheever's career through Bullet Park and contends
      that while he is "a shrewd observer of manners and morals" in
      his stories, his novels--except his first--have been failures.
      Argues that The Wapshot Scandal is "thesis-ridden" and that
      Bullet Park is "feeble." Concludes that "Cheever does not
      have the intellectual powers and the intensity of imagination
      to sustain a long fiction." Includes brief biography and
      primary bibliography.

5 FETTER, E. "Die Erfolgswelt des Eliot Nailles" [The successful
      world of Eliot Nailles]. Nationalzeitung (East Germany),
      12 November.
         Review of Bullet Park. Describes the novel as a partly
      drab, yet partly brilliant mosaic of an affluent world,
      behind which fear of life, hatred of existence, contempt for
      mankind, and flight into madness, dreams, drink, or drugs
      lurk ever-present.

6 GAUNT, MARCIA ELIZABETH. "Imagination and Reality in the Fiction
      of Katherine Anne Porter and John Cheever: Implications for
      Curriculum." Ph.D. dissertation, Purdue University, 174 pp.
         Contends that Cheever reconciles "imagination and reality
      primarily through irony." Contrasts Porter's more affirmative
      irony with Cheever's defeatist irony to provide "germinal in-
      sights for teaching and responding to literature."

7 HARMSEL, HENRIETTA TEN. "'Young Goodman Brown' and "'The Enormous
      Radio.'" Studies in Short Fiction 9 (Fall): 407-8.
         Differing with Burton Kendle [1967.5], Harmsel draws a
      parallel between Hawthorne's Brown and Cheever's Westcotts.
      Compares the "innocent" protagonists in each story, the decep-
      tive facades of their surroundings, and the dilemma each must
      face at the end.

1972

8 PROFFER, CARL R., ed. and trans. <u>Soviet Criticism of American</u>
   <u>Literature in the Sixties: An Anthology</u>. Ann Arbor: Ardis
   Publishers, pp. 23-26, 63, passim.
       Reprints of 1965.15; 1970.6.

9 REINHARDT, JAMES M. "Literary Criminology: Guilt and Despair
   in Murderers." <u>International Journal of Offender Therapy and</u>
   <u>Comparative Criminology</u> 16, no. 2: 160-70.
       Quotes from Cheever's "Torch Song" to illustrate that Kafka,
   Caldwell, Camus, and Cheever all evoke "exciting and fugitive
   moods and passions" when dealing with "the dark levels of grim
   despair and human tragedy."

10 REINHOLD, ROBERT. "Academy Split over Plan to Honour Ezra
    Pound." <u>Times</u> (London), 6 July, p. 6.
        Mentions Cheever is a member of the committee that nomi-
    nated Pound for the annual Emerson-Thoreau medal of the
    American Academy of Arts and Sciences.

11 SHEPARD, RICHARD F. "Yevtushenko Criticizes Journalists in Talk
    Here." <u>New York Times</u>, 22 January, p. 27.
        Mentions that Cheever was among the guests at the New
    School's Graduate Faculty Center, where Yevgeny Yevtushenko
    received an honorary degree.

12 TODD, RICHARD. "Gathering at Bunnymede." <u>Atlantic Monthly</u> 229
    (January): 86-88.
        Notes that Cheever attended <u>Playboy</u>'s International
    Writers' Convocation in October 1971.

1973

1 ALGREN, NELSON. "Roth, DeVries, Colter, Cheever: Feasting on
   Fiction." <u>Chicago Tribune Book World</u>, 13 May, pp. 1, 3.
       Review of <u>The World of Apples</u>. Maintains that Cheever,
   like Hawthorne, shares "a heritage of Puritan demons, as well
   as the necessity of exorcising them thru [sic] writing." In
   Cheever's fiction, the primal sin "is to lose touch with the
   human condition." <u>The World of Apples</u>, despite Cheever's re-
   assuring preface, "is not one of those promising and prettily-
   wrapped Saroyanish packages," but has only a surface innocence,
   like Nathaniel West's, which conceals "hellish meanings."

2 ANON. Review of <u>The World of Apples</u>. <u>Booklist</u> 69 (1 July):
   1007.
       Notes that Cheever's characters in this collection "ex-
   perience dramatic misunderstandings as they cope with life."

3 ANON. Review of <u>The World of Apples</u>. <u>Choice</u> 10 (October): 1190.
Finds that this collection reveals Cheever "at his best."
Notes that he is "an elegant stylist," who conveys "the com-
plexity and terror of life" while keeping in mind that, besides being desperate, life can also be quite funny.

4 ANON. Review of <u>The World of Apples</u>. <u>Kirkus Reviews</u> 41, no. 5:
266.
Does not find these stories as memorable as "The Country
Husband" or "The Swimmer"; yet notes the familiar presence
of "the bitter lemon of nostalgia, the affectionate and truly
moral concern, and above all that skewed element of surprise."

5 ANON. Review of <u>The World of Apples</u>. <u>Publishers Weekly</u> 203
(12 March): 73.
Publication announcement.

6 ANON. "Academy of Arts Elects Six." <u>New York Times</u>,
10 December, p. 58.
Reports that Cheever and five others were elected "last
week" to membership in the American Academy of Arts and
Letters.

7 ANON. "The Best and the Brightest, 1973." <u>Washington Post Book
World</u>, 9 December, pp. 1-2.
Lists <u>The World of Apples</u> among the year's best books and
notes that in this collection "memory is the chief force,
quaintness and innocence the basic values; violence is subdued in nostalgia."

8 ANON. "Briefly Noted: Fiction." <u>Washington Post Book World</u>,
13 May, p. 15.
Notes publication of <u>The World of Apples</u>.

9 ANON. "The New Yorker Lists at This Season Some Books by its
Contributors Published during the Year." <u>New Yorker</u> 49
(3 December): 192.
Includes <u>The World of Apples</u> and notes that Cheever's
"matter-of-fact tone" does not prepare the reader for what
is coming.

10 ANON. "A Selection of the Year's Best Books." <u>Time</u> 102
(31 December): 56.
Lists <u>The World of Apples</u> and comments that "the Bullfinch
of the U.S. middle class effects some unsettling awakenings
from the American Dream."

1973

11 BAZERMAN, CHARLES. "Victories of Happy Madness." Nation 217
    (10 September): 218-19.
        Review of The World of Apples. Considers these stories
    as typical of modern American tragic fiction and notes that
    they appeal to the morose part of the contemporary reader,
    who is "convinced that we will soon end up fat, crazy or
    dead."

12 CROMIE, ROBERT. "Book Beat." Public Broadcasting Service, May.
        Interview. A thirty-minute telecast in which Cheever dis-
    cusses The World of Apples.

13 DEEMER, CHARLES. "Old Masters' New Stories." New Leader 56
    (17 September): 19-20.
        Review of The World of Apples. Finds that Cheever's wit,
    at its best, combines "humor and acerbity." "The Chimera"
    best illustrates that "Cheever's is a domain without redemp-
    tion." Reprinted: 1975.4.

14 De FEO, RONALD. "Cheever Underachieving." National Review 25
    (11 May): 536-37.
        Review of The World of Apples. Finds that this collection
    reflects no real growth in Cheever's work since The Brigadier
    and the Golf Widow, and the current book "seems rather tired"
    in comparison to the earlier volume. Even the most successful
    stories, "The Jewels of the Cabots" and "Percy," "don't have
    much bite." Suspects that now Cheever is "so confident in
    his abilities that he has grown too casual."

15 EDWARDS, THOMAS R. "Surprise, Surprise." New York Review of
    Books, 17 May, pp. 35-36.
        Review of The World of Apples. Discusses at length and
    praises the title story as "virtually flawless" and finds
    that it stands out from what is "an otherwise uneven and
    rather tired collection." In this story, as in other of
    Cheever's best work, "there is usually more life lurking
    than he or the reader can quite cope with." But most of the
    stories here tend to be dull and simply "lapse into mannerism,"
    or at best, smugness, and it is there that Cheever seems to be
    taking "easy ways out." Reprinted: 1977.60.

16 HASSAN, IHAB. "American Literature." In World Literature Since
    1945, edited by Ivar Ivask and Gero von Wilpert, pp. 18, 26.
    New York: Frederick Ungar.
        Notes that Cheever is a "more benign" satirist than Mary
    McCarthy and that his Wapshot novels are American in their
    "generosities" and "also human in [their] dalliance with
    fate."

17 _____. "Radical Innocence: Studies in the Contemporary American
Novel. Princeton, N.J.: Princeton University Press.
Paperback reprint of 1961.18.

18 KAZIN, ALFRED. Bright Book of Life: American Novelists and
Storytellers from Hemingway to Mailer. Boston: Little,
Brown, pp. 110-14.
Describes Cheever's stories as "a demonstration of the
amazing sadness, futility and evanescence" of suburban life.
Finds that one does not care about the fate of the various
characters: "It is Cheever one watches in the story." Re-
printed: 1974.7; 1975.4.

19 _____. "O'Hara, Cheever & Updike." New York Review of Books,
19 April, pp. 14-18.
Finds that although Cheever "found in suburbsville almost
as many cruel social differences as O'Hara," Cheever's stories
have gone beyond slice-of-life realism and become demonstra-
tions "of the amazing sadness, futility, and evanescence of
life among the settled, moneyed . . . people in Proxmire
Manor." Describes Cheever as an "intellectual," whose "mar-
velous brightness is an effort to cheer himself up."

20 LEHMANN-HAUPT, CHRISTOPHER. "In Defense of John Cheever." New
York Times, 10 May, p. 43.
Review of The World of Apples. Admits that Cheever at
times "indulges in forced whimsicality and determined eccentricity"; yet finds that the beauty of this collection as a
whole is better than its best parts. Sees the title story as
the "key to this beauty," revealing Cheever as "our most
telling explorer of the geography of the heart."

21 LEMON, LEE T. "Working Quietly." Prairie Schooner 47 (Fall):
270.
Review of The World of Apples. Although these stories are
of high quality overall and are "quietly appealing," some of
them are annoying because of "Cheever's penchant for creating
talkative narrators who tell the readers more than they want
or need to know."

22 LEONARD, JOHN. "Cheever to Roth to Malamud." Atlantic Monthly
231 (June): 112-16.
Review of The World of Apples. Calls Cheever "a Chekhov
of the exurbs" and considers this collection, like the rest
of his fiction, an examination of the "failure of reciprocity
in our relations with the rest of the universe." Finds these
stories sustained by Cheever's careful irony, which still
manages to preserve love and humor. Reprinted: 1975.4.

1973

23 _____. "1973: An Apology and 38 Consolations." <u>New York Times</u>
<u>Book Review</u>, 2 December, p. 2.
Lists <u>The World of Apples</u> among the "significant" books of
1973.

24 MADDOCKS, MELVIN. "Big-Wheelbase Literature Must Go."
<u>Christian Science Monitor</u>, 7 May, p. 9.
Praises the short story form for its "concentrated excitement" and "an electric perception" matched by only a few
novels. Cites <u>The World of Apples</u> as exemplary of this
"minority" form and describes the collection as a "matchless
source book," which demonstrates the decency, and its limits,
of the middle class.

25 _____. "Crabgrass in Eden." <u>Time</u> 101 (21 May): 99–100.
Review of <u>The World of Apples</u>. Praises Cheever's polished,
lyrical sentences and finds that these stories are "at the
very top" of the short story genre. Notes that since his
suburbia can no longer contain the "maddened lovers" and
"wild death haters, . . . Cheever appears to be reaching
deeper into his imagination, exploring new and more perilous
provinces."

26 MANO, D. KEITH. "The World of Apples." <u>Washington Post Book</u>
<u>World</u>, 1 July, pp. 1, 10.
Review of <u>The World of Apples</u>. Feels that Cheever's concern with memory is unrivaled among writers since Proust, and
throughout this collection, his characters seem to be "remembered posthumously while they are alive." This focus on
retrospection is a "sharp repudiation of realism" and in
this "age of Tom Wolfe . . . is heroic." Reprinted: 1975.4.

27 McCULLOUGH, DAVID. "Eye on Books." <u>Book-of-the-Month Club News</u>,
July, pp. 6–7.
Review of <u>The World of Apples</u>. Finds this book "one of the
most humane books of the season." Includes a brief biographical sketch of Cheever and a number of his comments on his
writing. Cheever explains that he finds the short story form
"very accommodating," because he never knows "where my characters come from or where they are going."

28 MUDRICK, MARVIN. "Old Pros with News from Nowhere." <u>Hudson</u>
<u>Review</u> 26 (Fall): 545–61.
Review of <u>The World of Apples</u>. Describes Cheever as an
"old pro" who manages in most of his short fiction "to veil
past, present, and future in a fine gray spittle of arbitrary
disillusion." Notes also that Cheever "has a thing about
pornography, and nearly loses his temper attacking it directly
in two of the stories."

29 NICOL, CHARLES. "Whistling Away The Dark." St. Louis Post-
    Dispatch, 3 June, p. 4-F.
        Review of The World of Apples. Finds that Cheever "is able
    to grasp some truths of our time and squeeze them until they
    yield." His stories here often concern "the loss of love"
    his protagonists experience, and of these "The Fourth Alarm"
    is "perhaps the best story in this collection."

30 OBERBECK, S. K. "Curdled Camelot." Newsweek 81 (21 May):
    97, 99.
        Review of The World of Apples. Finds that every story in
    this collection "is infused with quirky nostalgia, gentle
    mystery, melancholy fantasy."

31 PHILLIPS, ROBERT. Review of The World of Apples. Commonweal
    99 (30 November): 245-47.
        Contends that this collection "is as important to the
    Cheever canon as a carbon copy is to its bright original."
    Since Cheever writes only of one class, his work does not
    offer a "Balzacian cross-section of humanity." This book has
    more in common with the "somewhat trivial" The Way Some People
    Live than with "Cheever's best" collection, The Enormous
    Radio. Reprinted: 1976.9.

32 POWNAL, DAVID E. Articles on 20th Century Literature: An
    Annotated Bibliography. New York: Kraus-Thomson Organization,
    pp. 462-63.
        Annotates: 1963.2; 1964.15; 1964.27; 1969.11.

33 RABINOWITZ, DOROTHY. "Current Books in Short Compass." World
    2 (8 May): 53.
        Review of The World of Apples. Praises Cheever's deft and
    interesting style and notes that "the characters, like the
    plot, are secondary elements in this fiction, whose texture
    is all the story there is." Finds that whatever darkness
    certain of these characters may possess, Cheever has "the
    gift of sympathy" for them all. Reprinted: 1975.4.

34 RIDDLEY, CLIFFORD A. "Short Stories Extinct? Don't Believe It."
    National Observer, 2 June, p. 21.
        Review of The World of Apples. Finds that Cheever exults
    in the humanity of his characters, who struggle in a world
    where "home and family are but transient and ephemeral."
    Contends that as long as Cheever continues to write, the
    short story "will be around to delight and instruct us."

35 SIGGINS, CLARA M. Review of The World of Apples. Best Sellers
    33 (15 June): 136.

1973

Finds that this "great" collection depicts a world that is "almost emptied of all but dreams." Praises Cheever's "realistic dialogue" and notes that his men are better drawn than his women, who are either bitches or "dreamgirls." Concludes that Cheever has captured "much of the unease and meaninglessness of modern life."

36 VALHOULI, JAMES NICHOLAS. "John Cheever: The Dual Vision of His Art." Ph.D. dissertation, University of Wisconsin, 263 pp.
    Examines Cheever's style, themes, and world vision in his fiction through Bullet Park and considers "Cheever's thought about contemporary American life."

37 WAIN, JOHN. "Literate, Witty, Civilized." New Republic 168 (26 May): 24-26.
    Review of The World of Apples. Focuses on the title story, since it, most effectively in this collection, deals with the problem of finding meaning on a seemingly meaningless planet. Praises Cheever for his "bedrock and affirmative" quality, which enables him to create "people [who] behave as decently as they generally do in real life, rather than behaving like sick fiends," which is often the case in modern literature. Reprinted: 1976.9.

38 WIMBLE, BARTON L. Review of The World of Apples. Library Journal 98 (1 April): 1189-90.
    Finds that although Cheever is a "brilliant technician and unconventional wit" throughout these stories, he is unable to "sustain himself" after a few pages. He tends to lapse into irrelevant detail "or, more often, runs out of steam and simply brings the story to an end." The best piece here may well be the title story.

39 WOIWODE, L. "The World of Apples." New York Times Book Review, 20 May, pp. 1, 26.
    Review of The World of Apples. Describes this "extraordinary book" as a "transfiguring experience for the reader." Finds Cheever's prose to have the "oracular tone of a prophet" and compares him to Chekhov in his "gentility, ingenuous warmth, humor, universality" and in his knowing, yet forgiving treatment of human weakness. Reprinted: 1975.4.

40 WOLFE, GEOFFREY. "Cheever's Career Back in Focus with Apples." Los Angeles Times Book Review, 24 June, pp. 1, 10-11.
    Review of The World of Apples. Finds that Cheever's "accomplishment is huge; his talent is intimidating; his employment of his gift has been at times honest, . . . his work has dazzle and resonance and great depth." Provides synopses

for five of the stories and praises Cheever for his integrity
as a writer.

1974

1 ANON. "Forbidden Fruit." Times Literary Supplement 73
     (15 March): 253.
        Review of The World of Apples. Finds that "Cheever is
     cool, knowing and extremely funny" and that this collection
     "shows his eye and wit to be as bright as ever." Notes that
     Cheever is more successful on familiar ground, such as his
     stories of Americans in Italy. However, his description of
     the charter tour to Moscow "contains only the triter absurd-
     ities." Reprinted: 1977.60.

2 ANON. "Paperbacks of the Month." New York Times Book Review,
     9 June, p. 22.
        Review of The World of Apples. Notes its paperback pub-
     lication and quotes from 1973.39.

3 BLUMBERG, MYRNA. "Short Stories." Times (London), 4 April, p. 9.
        Review of The World of Apples. Focuses on the title story
     and finds that the "organic peace of mind" sought by the pro-
     tagonist may be found in Cheever's "earlier, urbane and some-
     times coy yarns."

4 GRAVES, NORA CALHOUN. "The Dominant Color in John Cheever's
     'The Swimmer.'" Notes on Contemporary Literature 4 (March):
     4-5.
        Traces the variants of the color green as they appear in
     association with the principal image of water and concludes
     that the change and range of colors parallels Merrill's
     refluence from his early "vigor and enthusiam" to "his
     contamination, growing insensitivity and personal erosion."

5 H[ALL], E[LIZABETH]. "Briefly." Psychology Today 8 (October):
     25.
        Review of The World of Apples. Describes these stories as
     "melancholy, nostalgic" and praises them for taking "just the
     right twist, often leading the reader into surprising byways."

6 HASSAN, IHAB. "Mid-century and After: Fiction." In Literary
     History of the United States, edited by Robert E. Spiller,
     Willard Thorp, Thomas H. Johnson, Henry Seidel Canby,
     Richard M. Ludwig, and William M. Gibson, pp. 1469-70.
     New York: Macmillan.
        Describes Cheever as a "benign" fantasist, mentions the
     Wapshot novels, and notes that Cheever's characters seem

1974

"sometimes deft caricatures, conveying the heartiness and
generosity of American manners, the gaminess of life itself."

7 KAZIN, ALFRED. Bright Book of Life: American Novelists and
   Storytellers from Hemingway to Mailer. New York: Dell,
   pp. 110-14.
        Paperback reprint of 1973.18.

8 MAGILL, FRANK N., ed. "John Cheever." In Cyclopedia of World
   Authors. Vol. I, p. 360. Englewood Cliffs, N.J.: Salem
   Press.
        Biographical essay with brief primary and secondary
   bibliographies.

9 McLELLAN, JOSEPH. "Paperbacks." Washington Post Book World,
   30 June, p. 4.
        Notes publication of the paperback reprint of The World of
   Apples.

10 NYE, ROBERT. "Of bugs and Burroughs." Manchester Guardian, 110
    (16 March): 23.
        Review of The World of Apples. Praises Cheever's stories
    for being "consistently good" for thirty years; yet finds that
    his "sprightly technique" is "rather overmuch in evidence."
    The exception here is the title story, which is "authentically
    poignant."

11 PACE, ERIC. "4 Short Fiction Works Among 110 Titles Contending
    for N.B.A." New York Times, 18 March, p. 26.
        Lists The World of Apples among the National Book Award
    contenders.

12 PEDEN, WILLIAM. "Fiction Chronicle." Sewanee Review 82 (Fall):
    712-29.
        Review of The World of Apples. Finds that in this collec-
    tion, "Cheever's method has loosened up considerably; it is
    more varied, more flexible," than his earlier collections.
    Notes that "The Jewels of the Cabots," with its controlled
    disasters, is "Cheever at his best." Considers Cheever, his
    sophistication notwithstanding, to be a "conventional moral-
    ist." Reprinted: 1977.60.

13 SAGE, LORNA. "Undoing the past." Observer (London), 10 March,
    p. 33.
        Review of The World of Apples. Contends that Cheever, in
    these "smooth, self-contained" stories, "relishes the bottom-
    less bathos of sweet home." His social satire has Borges-like
    metaphysical speculations, as is evident in such stories as
    "Mene, Mene, Tekel, Uphasrin."

1975

14 SLABEY, ROBERT M. "John Cheever: The 'Swimming' of America."
    Notre Dame Review 1 (1 March): 23-27.
        Seeing Cheever and Washington Irving as American writers
    "who find 'reality' at the crossroads of actuality and myth,"
    Slabey draws parallels between Neddy Merrill's swim ("The
    Swimmer") and Rip Van Winkle's sleep. Finds that the experi-
    ences of both "time-travellers" are engendered by a desire to
    escape the troubles of daily life. In depicting Neddy's
    crisis as one "shared by his culture," Cheever then "follows
    in the line of our fabulist and mythopoeic writers, participat-
    ing in . . . the creation of American Reality."

15 THEROUX, PAUL. "Critics' choice." Times (London), 28 November,
    p. IV.
        Finds that the "extremely funny" World of Apples was
    among the best books of 1974.

16 _____. "Treasons." New Statesman 87 (8 March): 334.
        Review of The World of Apples. Praises Cheever for not
    letting these stories "lapse into the grotesque or arabesque,
    [becoming] a kind of Borges of the suburbs." Instead, told
    by relaxed narrators, these stories are often compassionate,
    and where there is farce, it is "tempered with the poignant
    and the exact." In addition, with a story such as
    "Montraldo," it is "Cheever's special gift to be able to tame
    the fantastic with a hilariously patient examination of the
    surprises this planet throws in the path of his victimised
    characters." Reprinted: 1977.60.

17 WINK, JOHN HOWARD. "John Cheever and the Broken World." Ph.D.
    dissertation, University of Arkansas, 237 pp.
        Considers Cheever's fiction through Bullet Park in order
    to demonstrate "how it posits a 'broken world,'" in the sense
    of Hart Crane's poem, "The Broken Tower." Contends that
    Cheever's characters "search for something in life that can
    be broadly referred to as 'the visionary company of love.'"

1975

1 KALECHOFSKY, ROBERTA. "John Cheever." In Encyclopedia of World
    Literature in the 20th Century, edited by Frederick Ungar and
    Lina Mainiero. Vol. 4, pp. 73-74. New York: Frederick Ungar.
        Discusses Cheever's career through Bullet Park and finds
    that Cheever suggests "that social destiny is synonymous with
    domestic adjustment" and that Cheever elevates his subject
    "from the commonplace by lyricism and wit." Includes brief
    primary and secondary bibliographies.

1975

2 LITZ, A. WALTON. "The Short Story Today." In <u>Major American
   Short Stories</u>, p. 715. New York: Oxford University Press.
      Introduces "The World of Apples" (reprinted here) by
   noting how it "shows how a change of landscape can reinvig-
   orate" the conventional short story form. Includes twenty-
   three explanatory footnotes to the story, printed with the
   text (pp. 782-93).

3 PEDEN, WILLIAM. <u>The American Short Story: Continuity and Change,
   1940-1975</u>. Boston: Houghton Mifflin, pp. 30-39, passim.
      Revised and enlarged edition of 1964.51. Includes <u>The
   World of Apples</u>. Sees the stories of <u>The Brigadier and the
   Golf Widow</u> as perhaps among Cheever's best, notable especially
   for their variety. Through his wry and subtle stories, including his most recent, Cheever emerges as "one of the most
   perceptive and urbane commentators" writing today.

4 RILEY, CAROLYN, ed. "John Cheever." In <u>Contemporary Literary
   Criticism</u>. Vol. 3, pp. 105-9. Detroit: Gale Research
   Company.
      Reprints excerpts from: 1964.1; 1964.18; 1964.27;
   1965.10; 1973.13; 1973.18; 1973.22; 1973.26; 1973.33;
   1973.39.

5 UPDIKE, JOHN. "And Yet Again Wonderful." In <u>Picked-Up Pieces</u>,
   pp. 427-28. New York: Alfred A. Knopf.
      Reprint of 1969.47.

6 WAKEMAN, JOHN, ed. "John Cheever." In <u>World Authors: 1950-1970</u>,
   pp. 309-11. New York: H. W. Wilson.
      Surveys Cheever's critical reception through <u>Bullet Park</u>.
   Includes primary and brief secondary bibliographies.

<u>1976</u>

1 BANNON, BARBARA. Review of <u>Falconer</u>. <u>Publishers Weekly</u> 210
   (27 December): 56.
      Finds <u>Falconer</u> a "profoundly moving" novel that is essen-
   tially about "the Christian experience of life, death, hope."

2 DONALDSON, SCOTT. "The Machines in Cheever's Garden." In <u>The
   Changing Face of the Suburbs</u>, edited by Barry Schwartz,
   pp. 309-22, 336-37. Chicago: University of Chicago Press.
      Finds that Cheever is "the Jeremiah of our suburban age"
   of technological progress, because he uses the upper-middle
   class suburb "to exemplify the rootlessness and artificiality
   of contemporary life." Contrasts the pastoral contentment of
   St. Botolphs with the "shallow and despicable life-style" of
   suburbia, which leads to boredom and depression.

3 FRIEDBERG, MAURICE. "The U.S. in the U.S.S.R.: American
   Literature through the Filter of Recent Soviet Publishing
   and Criticism." Critical Inquiry 2 (Spring): 519-83.
      Mentions the Soviet reception of Cheever's work. Includes
   an appendix (p. 559) providing an abstract of this critical
   response, in which Cheever emerges as a "traditional" realist
   and a "humanist."

4 GALLOWAY, DAVID. "John Cheever." In The Encyclopedia Americana.
   Vol. 6, p. 359. New York: Americana Corporation.
      Discusses Cheever's career through 1964 and describes him
   as "a satirist, but an urbane and indulgent one."

5 GRANT, ANNETTE. "John Cheever: The Art of Fiction LXII."
   Paris Review 17 (Fall): 39-66.
      Interview. Cheever comments on the reception of his
   novels, his dislike of writing in Hollywood, his career and
   friendship with E. E. Cummings, and his fiction in general.

6 HAAS, RUDOLPH. "The Enormous Radio." In Die Amerikanische
   Short Story Der Gegenwart: Interpretationen, edited by Peter
   Freese, pp. 140-50. Berlin: E. Schmidt.
      Briefly surveys Cheever's career and traces a number of
   allusions to the work of T. S. Eliot and Dylan Thomas in "The
   Enormous Radio." Also finds "amazing parallels" between the
   story and Hawthorne's "Young Goodman Brown."

7 HEALY, MARSHA BURRIS. "Cheever the Fabulator: Experimental
   Technique in his Novels and Short Stories." Ph.D. dissertation, Tulane University, 206 pp.
      Contends that as Cheever's career developed, his style
   increasingly revealed "characteristics of 'fabulation' in
   the use of narrator, plot, form, language, symbols, allusions
   and myth." Also considers black humor and structuralism in
   Cheever's work through Bullet Park.

8 MOORE, STEPHEN C. "The Hero on the 5:42: John Cheever's Short
   Fiction." Western Humanities Review 30 (Spring): 147-52.
      Maintains that Cheever uses the conventions of New Yorker
   fiction to create stories that transcend "the conventions
   without quite violating them." The characters in Cheever's
   fiction are "mythic" and exaggerated, and while they seem
   real at first, they "move out of the conventions of middle-
   brow realistic fiction into another territory." Against a
   background of suburban wasteland, his characters "persist in
   attempting some definition of self when confronted with
   adversity." Reprinted: 1977.60.

1976

9 NYREN, DOROTHY; KRAMER, MAURICE; and KRAMER, ELAINE FIALKA, eds.
   "John Cheever." In <u>A Library of Literary Criticism: Modern</u>
   <u>American Literature</u>. Vol. IV, supplement, pp. 94–95. New
   York: Frederick Ungar.
      Reprint of excerpts from: 1970.9; 1971.2; 1973.31;
   1973.37. (Incorrectly identifies the author of 1973.31 as
   Roland Laird; the correct name is Robert Phillips.)

10 SEYMOUR-SMITH, MARTIN, ed. "John Cheever," In <u>Who's Who in 20th</u>
   <u>Century Literature</u>, p. 80. New York: Holt, Rinehart &
   Winston.
      Refers to Cheever as a "competent American fiction writer
   of the smooth <u>New Yorker</u> school."

11 WEBER, OLGA S., ed. <u>Literary and Library Prizes</u>. New York:
   R. R. Bowker, pp. 101, 160, 161, 169, 340, 341.
      Partial listing of Cheever's awards from 1951 through 1965.

<u>1977</u>

1 ACKROYD, PETER. "Organisation." <u>Spectator</u> 239 (16 July): 24.
      Review of <u>Falconer</u>. Argues that there is "a peculiarly
   American affability about Cheever's prose which suggests . . .
   that anyone could have written it." In addition, finds that
   Cheever substitutes "half-hearted, tatty and incomplete"
   religious imagery for feeling, and refuses to take his own
   characters seriously. Yet notes that the "ironic disparity
   between idea and reality" is explored cleverly in many
   directions.

2 ALLEN, BRUCE. "Dream Journeys." <u>Sewanee Review</u> 85 (Fall):
   694–95.
      Review of <u>Falconer</u>. Considers this novel "challenging,"
   though not difficult, "because Cheever is content to resolve
   Farragut's ethical dilemma by means of paradox." The novel
   itself, with its "haphazard structure," is not realistic, and
   though its protagonist is "unique in contemporary fiction,"
   the minor characters are simply "grotesques" acting in episodes that are "expressionistic distortions."

3 AMIEL, BARBARA. "Now, Perhaps, It Will Become Fashionable to
   Treat John Cheever Seriously." <u>Macleans</u> 90 (4 April): 78.
      Review of <u>Falconer</u>. Observes that although the setting of
   this novel, which Cheever has created with "breathtaking
   brilliance," is radically different from that of his previous
   work, "the specific weight of his writing remains unchanged."
   Cheever's depth in <u>Falconer</u> has always been present in his
   writing, "even in his olive-and-cocktail-circuit novels."

The chief difference with this present novel is simply that
Cheever "has learned how to make his unique vision 'fashionable' and accessible to the trends of our time."

4 ANON. Review of Falconer. Choice 14 (September): 857-58.
      Finds that in its use of the prison as "an emblem of the
   world," Falconer may well be Cheever's best novel; "it is
   certainly the most unified."

5 ANON. Review of Falconer. Kirkus Reviews 45 (1 January):
      9, 11-12.
      Praises Cheever's flexible prose and considers the novel
   to be "a strong fix--a statement of the human condition, a
   parable of salvation." Notes that with this novel, Cheever
   has far transcended "those cuticle-clipped lawns and chlori-
   nated swimming pools."

6 ANON. Review of Falconer. Publishers Weekly 212 (26 December):
      66.
      Synopsis of 1976.1. Announces paperback edition.

7 ANON. "Books." Playboy 24 (June): 26-27.
      Review of Falconer. Finds this novel "an extraordinarily
   elegant work." Notes that the second chapter, which may be
   the "most outstanding" one, was originally published in Playboy (January 1976).

8 ANON. "Books Briefly." The Progressive 41 (July): 44.
      Review of Falconer. Notes that Cheever captures prison
   life "pitilessly" and that the reactions of Farragut to the
   environment of Falconer "reflect the lack of human warmth
   which Cheever seems to believe is the most dreadful of all
   conditions."

9 ANON. "Fiction." Booklist 73 (1 February): 792.
      Review of Falconer. Describes this work as an "effective
   novel of stark realism" until the implausible last three pages.

10 ANON. "Notes on Current Books." Virginia Quarterly Review 53
      (Autumn): 136-37.
      Review of Falconer. Finds this novel "a metaphysical,
   metaphorical foray into the realm of quasi-religiosity."
   Faults Cheever for not knowing just what he was trying to
   achieve.

11 ANON. "Poet Calls on Americans to Boycott Sofia." Times
      (London), 23 March, p. 9D.

1977

Reports that Soviet poet Vladimir Kornilov appealed to John Cheever, John Updike, and Erskine Caldwell to withdraw their endorsement of a writers' conference in Sofia in protest of Soviet human rights violations.

12 BENJAMIN, ALINE. "Westchester Literally Has Storybook Charm." New York Times, 7 August, sect. 22, pp. 1, 14.
    Mentions Cheever as one of the writers of distinction, along with Irving, Cooper, and Poe, among others, who has found "sustenance and inspiration" in Westchester County.

13 BRESLIN, JOHN B. "Percy and Cheever: Prison as Prism." America 136 (12 March): 221-22.
    Review of Falconer. Suggests that Cheever's Ezekiel Farragut and Percy's Lancelot Lamar "represent the declining state of American gentry, North and South, respectively." Yet Falconer and Lancelot are distinguished by their focus, as indicated by their titles. With Cheever it is the prison and the involved relationships formed among its inmates rather than the prisoner which commands our attention. However, that Falconer tends to have many memorable individual episodes and set pieces makes the novel as a whole disjointed and "harder to keep in focus."

14 BROWN, MICHAEL DAVID. "The Books of Christmas: 2." Washington Post Book World, 11 December, p. 1.
    Lists Falconer among the books the editors have "especially liked." Praises Cheever's "cool eye and wry detachment."

15 BURR, DANIEL AARON. "Narrative Strategies in the Short Stories of John Cheever." Ph.D. dissertation, University of Notre Dame, 218 pp.
    Traces the progress of Cheever's use of narrative strategies from his first story through The World of Apples. Finds that a "fundamental change in Cheever's narrative strategies" occurred in Some People, Places, and Things That Will Not Appear in My Next Novel, where Cheever questioned "the conventions of realistic fiction." His subsequent two story collections "move further and further away from the delineation of social reality into an exploration of strange quests and imaginary visions that are the activities of characters no longer in contact with other people."

16 CHEEVER, SUSAN. "A Duet of Cheevers." Newsweek 89 (14 March): 68-70, 73.
    Interview. Cheever comments that his writing has improved over the years and that now his "prose is much closer to the substance." Discusses also his family and career, his marriage, Falconer, and his recovery from alcoholism.

17 CLARK, LINDLEY H., JR. "A Christmas Potpourri of Books." Wall
    Street Journal, 15 December, p. 20.
        Notes that while less than completely successful, Falconer
    is a "bold book, with high intentions."

18 CLEMONS, WALTER. "Cheever's Triumph." Newsweek 89 (14 March):
    61-62, 64, 67.
        Cover story. Discusses Falconer in detail and traces
    Cheever's life and career. Sees Falconer as Cheever's "most
    somber, best sustained long narrative" and as evidence that
    Cheever "has never been a documentary realist."

19 COALE, SAMUEL. John Cheever. New York: Frederick Ungar.
        Introductory study of Cheever's fiction that discusses his
    four novels and a number of his stories. Finds that "the emo-
    tional center" of Cheever's work "remains somewhat elusive"
    and contends that Cheever "seems to want his style to be both
    disarming and protective at once." Sees Falconer as Cheever's
    "clearest and most accomplished testament of faith."

20 COATES, DENNIS EDWARD. "The Novels of John Cheever." Ph.D.
    dissertation, Duke University, 271 pp.
        Contends that despite his deserved reputation as a short
    story writer, "Cheever's real importance derives as much from
    his novels as from his stories." Finds that the novels are
    "highly original" and "complex" and that all four of these
    works "share similar patterns of imagery." Argues also that
    Coverly Wapshot, "the composite character" of Hammer and
    Nailles, and Ezekiel Farragut "are overtly modeled on the
    author."

21 COSER, LEWIS A. "Culture and Society." Society 14 (July-August):
    85-87.
        Review of Falconer. Observes that while a central point of
    the novel is that prisoners "are largely incapable of estab-
    lishing secure relationships with each other," Cheever's por-
    trait of this loveless world is "relatively benign." Though
    he sees that there is something "profoundly rotten" about
    contemporary society, Cheever maintains at the end of this
    novel that society can still be redeemed.

22 COSTA, PETER. "The blue sky of novelist John Cheever." The
    Stars and Stripes, 5 June, p. 9.
        Interview. Cheever discusses the novel genre and contrasts
    it with New Journalism. Comments briefly on Falconer and
    notes that Saul Bellow, "when he accepted the Nobel Prize . . .
    was the first male American novelist to comport himself with
    dignity."

1977

23 CUNNINGHAM, JOHN R. "He Finds 'Hope' In Prison." The Pittsburgh
      Press, 20 March, p. J-7.
          Review of Falconer. Finds that this novel is an honest
      portrait of prison life and praises the "delicate craftmanship"
      with which Cheever "sheds light on a potentially dark and sor-
      did situation." Notes also that Cheever has created a "superb
      collection of supporting characters," who effectively contrib-
      ute to Farragut's development.

24 DAVIS, HOPE HALE. "Escape Within Walls." The New Leader 60
      (25 April): 14-15.
          Review of Falconer. Finds that although the characters and
      setting are not realistic, Cheever seems to use the prison
      context to celebrate life, notably "a life strictly without
      women." For once Cheever has created a world, albeit one
      where freedom is denied, from which the emasculative woman
      is banished. In his earlier work, married life "was so uni-
      versal a state that its unhappiness could be taken as a meta-
      phor for the sadness of the human condition." In Falconer
      the homosexual love affair between Farragut and Jody "is pre-
      sented as an idyll unmarred by the awkward actualities of love
      that Cheever has made so poignant elsewhere." Thus, Cheever
      may now be slyly offering the reader one of the "'alternative
      life styles'" in this novel. Reprinted: 1978.17.

25 DETWEILER, ROBERT. "John Cheever's Bullet Park: A World Beyond
      Madness." In Essays in Honour of Professor Tyrus Hillway,
      edited by Erwin A. Stürzl, pp. 6-32. Salzburg, Austria:
      Institut fur Englische Sprache und Literatur, University of
      Salzburg.
          Details the relationship between the rhetorical devices of
      Bullet Park and the novel's "elements of incongruity, perver-
      sion, and insanity." Finds also that the novel's "pervasive
      religious setting" reveals that Cheever has a Blakean vision.

26 DIDION, JOAN. "Falconer." New York Times Book Review,
      6 March, pp. 1, 22, 24.
          Sees Cheever striking a "note of 'homelessness'" in Falconer
      with "an almost liturgical intensity." While this theme of
      estrangement has been present in Cheever's fiction before,
      it has previously concerned characters "exiled merely by their
      own errors or passions or foolishness." Falconer, however, is
      Cheever's "meditation on the abstraction Cheever has always
      called 'home' but has never before located in the life of the
      spirit." Reprinted: 1978.17.

27 FIRTH, JOHN. "Talking with John Cheever." Saturday Review 4
      (2 April): 22-23.

Interview. Cheever expresses his satisfaction with
Falcoer, discusses its theme, and comments on his keeping
a daily journal and on his life in Ossining.

28 FLOWER, DEAN. "Fiction Chronicle." Hudson Review 30 (Summer):
310-11.
Review of Falconer. Notes that after searching for an
appropriate form throughout his career, he has at last found
it in Falconer. Finds the climactic conclusion moving and
considers the novel itself the most profound and confident
Cheever has yet written.

29 FREEMONT-SMITH, ELIOT. "Books for the Long, Hot Summer: One
Critic's Choices." Village Voice 22 (27 June): 56.
Notes that Falconer is a "metaphysical novel" that is
moving, although it does not "haunt in the way that was perhaps intended." Describes Cheever's prose as "acute, precise,
coiled."

30 F[REEMONT]-S[MITH], E[LIOT]. "The Last Roundup." Village
Voice 22 (26 December): 75.
Lists Falconer among the National Book Critics Circle
award nominees. Describes the novel as "outwardly spare
but resonant with symbolic connections."

31 FRIEDBERG, MAURICE. A Decade of Euphoria: Western Literature in
Post-Stalin Russia, 1954-64. Bloomington: University of
Indiana Press, pp. 198-99.
Notes that since Cheever's introduction to Soviet readers
in 1961, with the publication of "The Superintendant," he has
continued to be published there.

32 FULLER, EDMUND. "Two Bold but Unsatisfying Novels." Wall Street
Journal, 12 April, p. 20.
Review of Falconer. Finds that despite Cheever's "high
intentions," Falconer "falls below his mark, in part as a
result of the excesses characteristic of the age." Observes
that the novel lacks focus, because Cheever so overplays his
theme of degradation that Farragut's plight "seems highly contrived, too synthetic."

33 GARDNER, JOHN. "On Miracle Row." Saturday Review 4 (2 April):
20-23.
Review of Falconer. Sees Cheever as "one of the few living
American novelists who might quality as true artists" and
finds Falconer "an extraordinary work of art." Praises
Cheever's ability to depict life's "pathos and beauty" without making excuses, because "what he says seems true"; he is
a great writer.

1977

34 GASTER, ADRIAN, ed. "John Cheever." <u>International Authors and</u>
    <u>Writers Who's Who</u>, 8th ed. Cambridge: Biographical Centre,
    pp. 178-79.
       Lists Cheever's publications and some awards through 1965.

35 GROTH, JANET. "Cheers for Cheever." <u>Commonweal</u> 104 (10 June):
    374-76.
       Review of <u>Falconer</u>. Contends that despite the Old Testa-
    ment allusions and allegorical aspects of the story, <u>Falconer</u>
    is not allegory; instead, Cheever "has incorporated into the
    novel a symbolic richness usually associated with deeply
    imaged poetry." By this and his admixture of "the sacred and
    profane he is reminiscent of John Donne." Argues, further,
    that <u>Falconer</u> is "a stunning meditation on all forms of con-
    finement and liberation that can be visited upon the human
    spirit." Reprinted: 1978.17.

36 HARDWICK, ELIZABETH. "An Exchange on Fiction." <u>New York Review</u>
    <u>of Books</u>, 3 February, pp. 44-45.
       Reply to Cheever's published letter (p. 44), which criti-
    cized Hardwick's essay "A Sense of the Present" for the view
    that the modern novel is "overwhelmed by the complexities of
    contemporary life."

37 H[ARRISON], K[EITH]. "Novels." <u>The Carleton Miscellany</u> 17
    (Winter): 145.
       Review of <u>Falconer</u>. Describes the novel as "the most over-
    rated book of the year." Finds Farragut "unconvincing" and
    the number of coincidences "just too much."

38 HELLER, AMANDA. "Short Views." <u>Atlantic Monthly</u> 239 (April):
    91.
       Review of <u>Falconer</u>. Finds that the novel is "both bizarre
    and touchingly real, absolutely beautiful." Considers the
    source of <u>Falconer</u>'s dramatic appeal as arising from Cheever's
    artful confrontation of the nightmare of incarceration. Re-
    printed: 1978.17.

39 HERMAN, JAN. "John Cheever Never Plays Celebrity Role." <u>Chicago</u>
    <u>Sun-Times</u>, 17 April, "Show" sect., pp. 1, 9.
       Interview. Cheever comments on his relationship with the
    writers of his generation, gives his views on literature, and
    defines fiction as "a complex distillation of reality, anxi-
    ety and aspiration." Discusses his own writing regimen and
    lists some of the "prerequisites for being a novelist."

40 HERSEY, JOHN. "John Hersey Talks With John Cheever." <u>Yale</u>
    <u>Alumni Magazine and Journal</u> (December): 21-24.

Interview. Cheever discusses his education, family, and some of the older writers he knew. Mentions Falconer and comments at length on nostalgia, which, he explains, "is very much a part of my life." Reprinted: 1978.45.

41 _____. "Talk With John Cheever." New York Times Book Review, 6 March, pp. 1, 24, 26-28.
Interview. Cheever discusses Falconer and refers to his teaching at Sing Sing. Mentions Chekhov and comments on his being "a liturgical churchgoer," his physical health, his immediate family, and the "darkness and radiance" of Falconer.

42 IYER, PICO. "A Nice Reliable Chevrolet: Aspects of John Cheever." London Magazine 17 (November), 41-48.
Review of Falconer. Contends that Cheever is "colourless, spare, and reliably, fantastically efficient as a writer." Notes that his "especial talent is precisely his lack of brilliance, his retreat from the bright . . . into the . . . banal." Falconer itself is a moving, "fine book, but it is often fine by default, succeeding more through its sterilisa-tion of flaws than its gathering of felicities." Compares Cheever's achievement, in kind, to "Wordsworth's focus upon the small, the common and the sublime" and argues that as a "non-Jewish, non-intellectual writer renowned for his normal-ity," Cheever may well be "the Great American Novelist, if all the emphasis of that title falls upon the middle word."

43 KAZIN, ALFRED. "Letters." New York Times Book Review, 10 April, p. 37.
Letter to the editor in response to Joan Didion's criti-cism (1977.26) of Kazin's view of "The Country Husband."

44 KERMODE, FRANK. "Porridge in America." The Listener 98 (7 July): 30.
Review of Falconer. Contends that despite the episodic narrative, the novel "is a remarkably articulated fictional meditation on imprisonedness." Still, it lacks "that author-ity . . . that we associate with the best," even though it is "stronger than the earlier work" of Cheever.

45 KORT, WESLEY A. "Access to Wisdom." Christian Century 94 (6 July): 633-34.
Review of Falconer. Focuses on that great amount of pres-sure "put on the element of character" in this novel and finds that this work stands in the current of such American fiction as The Narrative of Arthur Gordon Pym, Walden, and The Red Badge of Courage.

1977

46 KREBS, ALBIN. "Notes on People." <u>New York Times</u>, 1 January,
    p. 12.
        Mentions that Cheever has been named to the board of the
    American Academy and Institute of Arts and Letters.

47 LARDNER, SUSAN. "Miscreants." <u>New Yorker</u> 53 (2 May): 141-42.
        Review of <u>Falconer</u>. Finds that like Farragut's escape
    from prison, Cheever's style "is an excursion among the flora
    and fauna of the rain forest, a circumvention of edifying
    logic, an evasion of straight answers." Although he takes
    risks with words like "transcendence," "mystery," and "pro-
    fundity," Cheever is able to avoid "absurdity, sometimes nar-
    rowly, by hanging on to physical details."

48 LEHMANN-HAUPT, CHRISTOPHER. "Ceremonies of Guilt." <u>New York
    Times</u>, 3 March, p. 31.
        Review of <u>Falconer</u>. Sees the disjointed plot of <u>Falconer</u>
    as a "riot of surrealistic fragments." Finds the first eighty
    pages a "subliminal nightmare," while the remainder of the
    novel "is somehow redemptive." The effect is disturbing and
    genuine and the novel is "extraordinary."

49 LEONARD, JOHN. "Crying in the Wilderness." <u>Harper's</u> 254
    (April): 88-89.
        Review of <u>Falconer</u>. Finds that "Cheever has left Shady
    Hill in a black van through the twilight zone and into hell."
    Argues that although absorbing, it is ultimately confusing
    for the protagonist to have wandered into this novel from the
    world of Kafka or Celine. Reprinted: 1978.17.

50 LEVINSON, DANIEL. Review of <u>Falconer</u>. <u>Library Journal</u> 102
    (1 February): 403.
        Finds that Cheever's prison setting is a "potent metaphor"
    for his theme of alienation in modern society. Praises
    Cheever's use of irony, which allows him to present familiar
    scenes "through a characteristically brilliant warp."

51 LEWIS, JEREMY. "Fiction." <u>Times</u> (London), 7 July, p. 19.
        Review of <u>Falconer</u>. Laments the lack of "vitality" in
    <u>Falconer</u> and numbers Cheever among "the more flatulent Amer-
    ican novelists," one who must demonstrate that he is both
    "compassionate and profound."

52 LOCKE, RICHARD. "Novelists as Preachers." <u>New York Times Book
    Review</u>, 17 April, pp. 3, 52-53.
        Sees the "symbolic Christian realism" of <u>Falconer</u> as part
    of a trend in contemporary fiction to write moral fables.
    However, writers such as Cheever, Percy, Didion, and Berger

at their worst "cease being novelists and become embittered preachers, moralists who stack the deck." Describes Falconer as forceful but ultimately "unimpressive." Reprinted: 1978.17.

53 McELROY, JOSEPH. "Falconer by John Cheever." New Republic 176 (26 March): 31-32.
  Praises Cheever for allowing his style to coincide with the protagonist's "groping pain and strength."

54 McKINLEY, JAMES. "Falconer: Parable, Not Sermon." National Catholic Reporter 13 (15 April): 14.
  Sees the prison setting of Falconer as a parable of the soul being imprisoned in the body of Farragut. Cheever's writing is "clear and clean," and his treatment of the reconciliation of the flesh with the spirit is done with "admirable sensitivity."

55 McPHERSON, WILLIAM. "Lives in a Cell." Washington Post Book World, 20 March, pp. 1-2.
  Review of Falconer. Contends that the subject matter of "this moving and excellent novel" does not represent a departure from Cheever's earlier work, since he consistently observes life "with the same cool eye" and describes it "in the same clear prose." Praises Cheever for taking risks in writing this novel.

56 MAGILL, FRANK N., ed. Survey of Contemporary Literature. Englewood Cliffs, N.J.: Salem Press, pp. 929-30, 964-67, 3557-59, 8076-79, 8080-86, 8407-10.
  Provides synopses of The Brigadier and the Golf Widow, Bullet Park, The Housebreaker of Shady Hill, The Wapshot Chronicle, The Wapshot Scandal, and The World of Apples.

57 MANO, D. KEITH. "Exhaustion." National Review 29 (22 July): 833-34.
  Review of Falconer. Contends that his novel is "Cheever upside down"; evil here is expressed, not expressionist, as in his work. In Falconer Cheever has left the eccentricity of the eighteenth century and entered the twentieth century. Previously, "Cheever has been a guardian to his readers"; in Falconer, there is "sordidness and human ignobility," and this may well be Cheever's last novel, since it reflects his exhaustion.

58 MARCUS, GREIL. "The Literary Con Game." Rolling Stone, 2 June, p. 85.

1977

> Review of <u>Falconer</u>. Notes that this novel is "not a dis-
> honest book, but it's not a good one either." Finds that the
> book's warm critical reception is due less to its strength
> than to its seriousness, which stands in contrast to his
> earlier, "lighter chronicles of American suburban life."

59 MEISEL, PERRY. "Cheever's Challenge: Find Freedom." <u>Village
     Voice</u> 22 (21 March): 74, 76.
> Review of <u>Falconer</u>. Finds what Cheever has to say here is
> "sobering and impressive." Despite its tendency toward
> Miltonic theology, the novel is "much bigger than its theol-
> ogy." The two currents of the novel, "one humanist, one
> cybernetic--meet to generate the complexities of <u>Falconer</u>
> as a whole." It is a mark of Cheever's achievement that
> these worlds are in harmony and that they find their correla-
> tive in the prison itself.

60 MENDELSON, PHYLLIS C. and BRYFONSKI, DEDRIA, eds. "John
     Cheever." In <u>Contemporary Literary Criticism</u>. Vol. 7,
     pp. 48-50. Detroit: Gale Publishing Company.
> Reprint of excerpts from 1969.47; 1971.1; 1973.15;
> 1974.1; 1974.12; 1974.16; 1976.8.

61 MUNRO, ELEANOR. "Not Only I the Narrator, but I John Cheever."
     <u>Ms.</u>, 5 (April): 74-77, 105.
> Interview. Cheever comments on his life and the role of
> nostalgia in his writings and briefly discusses <u>Falconer</u>'s
> prison metaphor of confinement. Talks also about his women
> characters and gives his views on fiction written by women.

62 NORDELL, RODERICK. "<u>Falconer</u>: Cheever's Latest." <u>Christian
     Science Monitor</u>, 30 March, p. 27.
> Review of <u>Falconer</u>. Finds that the prison world of the
> novel is "a metaphor of bounded existence, somewhat like one
> of Cheever's suburbs." Despite the novel's "positive thrust,"
> <u>Falconer</u> is flawed by "the deadening four-letter words" and by
> the importance Cheever gives to "'unsavory matters.'" Notes
> also that unlike his Old Testament namesake, Ezekiel Farragut
> "slips into idealizing, and even participating in, the abomi-
> nations he witnesses," instead of insisting on repentance "as
> the price of escape."

63 OATES, JOYCE CAROL. "An Airy Insubstantial World." <u>Ontario
     Review</u> 7 (Fall-Winter): 99-101.
> Review of <u>Falconer</u>. Views the novel as "a fable, a kind
> of fairy tale; near-structureless, it has the feel of an
> assemblage of short stories, and is consequently most success-
> ful in fragments: in patches of emotion." Despite occasional

"striking passages," the novel is ultimately a disappointment: "its transcendence of genuine pain and misery is glib, even crude."

64 OLSON, CLARENCE E. "Cellblock of the Mind." St. Louis Post-Dispatch, 6 March, p. 4-B.
      . Review of Falconer. Describes the novel as "a 'heady' book," in that it "explores the strange power of the mind to summon up unwilled the images, sounds and smells of a past that may or may not have existed." Suggests also that Cheever's ability to recreate the loss of physical and mental control that accompanies alcoholism and drug use may be attributed to the author's personal experience.

65 ROMANO, JOHN. "Redemption According to Cheever." Commentary 63 (May): 66-69.
      Review of Falconer. Although Cheever reveals his belief in redemption and spiritual renewal, his lament of the fallen world is in the tradition of Yeats, Eliot, and Robert Lowell. Notes that the puzzling moral outcome is clearly a Christian allegory concerning the importance of love and sympathy. However, as much as the novel may be a moving one, because of Cheever's imbalance in favor of sympathy over creative imagination, Falconer is "artistically soft."

66 SAGE, LORNA. "Escape via Heaven." Observer (London), 10 July, p. 24.
      Review of Falconer. Praises Cheever for going "for the hard stuff" by taking chances in this "shamelessly ambitious, funny novel." Finds that Cheever "has the nerve to leave the emotions vulnerable," instead of glossing his material with "protective irony."

67 SHEPPARD, R. Z. "View from the Big House." Time 109 (28 February): 79-80.
      Review of Falconer. Finds that Farragut is "an undeniably Cheeverish" character, bearing the legacy of his old New England family. The novel itself is emotionally charged but loosely structured, and the protagonist's own sententiousness makes the reader feel "as if the novel itself were a correctional institution." Cheever is strongest here when conveying a sense of "mortal illness that must be overcome." Since the novel ends by emphasizing that survival itself is always a miracle and its own reward, Falconer may well be viewed as "not a young man's book."

68 SPECTOR, ROBERT D. "Review of Falconer. World Literature Today 51 (Autumn): 619.

1977

Contends that despite its "terse narrative structure," its
economy of language, and its carefully crafted style, "Falconer
is a disappointing novel." Sees its values as "blurred" and
its characters as unable to evoke "sympathy or interest." In
fact, the protagonist is "unattractive and unreliable," and
there are "some lapses into incredible dialogue."

69 SYMONS, JULIAN. "Soul behind bars." Times Literary Supplement
      76 (8 July): 821.
        Review of Falconer. Finds this novel lively, though at
    times "a little sloppy, sometimes comic and occasionally
    rather contrivedly horrific." Laments that Cheever is the
    "quintessentially New Yorker writer," combining an admirable
    style without "much awareness of how people actually live or
    behave." Argues that the novel teaches an old lesson: "to
    mix realism and fantasy is almost always not only dangerous
    but damaging." Although Falconer, which is at times over-
    written, is interesting and talented, it is able to be called
    a masterpiece only because of "the communal madness that seems
    sometimes to afflict American critics." Reprinted: 1978.17.

70 T[AURIG], A[LFRED]. Review of Falconer. West Coast Review of
      Books 3 (May): 30.
        Finds that in its understated recitation of prison horrors,
    Falconer "is a savage indictment of the 'reform'-minded sys-
    tem." The novel is compelling, despite its tendency to ram-
    ble in a "semi-stream of consciousness narration of events."

71 TOSCHES, NICK. "When Literary Lights Turn On the TV." New York
      Times, 25 December, p. 29.
        Surveys the favorite television programs of a number of
    literary figures and finds that Cheever bought a set "about
    a week ago" and so far has watched PBS' "Nova" and "Monday
    Night Football." Describes these programs as "both great."

72 TOWERS, ROBERT. "Up the River." New York Review of Books,
      17 March, pp. 3-6.
        Review of Falconer. Finds that this is a "surprising"
    novel that "edges into surrealism" and is distinguished from
    Cheever's previous work by its atmosphere of "extreme sordid-
    ness." Yet, as with even his earliest fiction, Falconer deals
    with "the precariousness of life" and its characters are as
    manipulated as ever. Concludes that Falconer, despite its
    flaws, is compelling "as the darkened realization of much
    that has been implicit in Cheever's fiction all along."
    Reprinted: 1978.17.

73 TREGLOWN, JEREMY. "Gaol Bait." <u>New Statesman</u> 94 (15 July):
      p. 91.
          Review of <u>Falconer</u>. Finds that Cheever effectively traces
      Farragut's "appalling emotional adaptability." Compares this
      novel to Kesey's <u>One Flew Over the Cuckoo's Nest</u> and finds
      that in each author's treatment of the problems of penal and
      mental institutions, "Cheever is more honest, and the hope-
      lessness of trying to arbitrate between a self-absorbed,
      hypocritical murderer and an insulated, savage, feebly-
      supervised penal administration . . . comes across with real,
      if intermittent force."

74 TYLER, ANNE. "Chocolates in the Afternoon and Other Temptations
      of a Novelist." <u>Washington Post Book World</u>, 4 December, p. 3.
          Lists <u>Falconer</u> among the new works of fiction "compelling
      enough to read in the daytime." Finds that the novel was
      "often disturbing" but that "something luminous about it made
      me feel profoundly hopeful."

75 _____. "Life in Prison With a Sunny Innocent." <u>National</u>
      <u>Observer</u> 16 (12 March): 19.
          Review of <u>Falconer</u>. Sees Farragut as another of Cheever's
      "confused, lonely men," except he has "finally fallen through
      the ice." <u>Falconer</u>'s elements of fantasy provide the fitting
      vehicle for the forces that confine the human spirit, and the
      novel as a whole perfectly concentrates "all that is wonderful
      and sad and astonishing in everyday life."

76 WADE, ROSALIND. "Quarterly Fiction Review." <u>Contemporary</u>
      <u>Review</u> 231 (October): 214-15.
          Review of <u>Falconer</u>. Finds the opening scene of the novel
      the most effective, with the least convincing scene occurring
      at the end: Farragut's escape. In between, the novel pre-
      sents an accurate and unforgettable, if grisly and "off-beat"
      revelation of prison life, "despite discrepancies, inconsis-
      tencies and occasional crudities."

77 WEAVER, JOHN D. "John Cheever: Recollections of a Childlike
      Imagination." <u>Los Angeles Times Book Review</u>, 13 March,
      pp. 3, 8.
          Traces his friendship with Cheever from their meeting in
      December 1943. Reprints extracts of letters Cheever has writ-
      ten and notes that Cheever "goes through life with a winning
      lottery ticket in his pocket, confident that at any moment
      someone will ring up to check the lucky number."

78 WHITMAN, ALDEN. "John Cheever's Morality Play for Moderns."
      <u>Los Angeles Times Book Review</u>, 13 March, pp. 1, 8.

1977

Review of Falconer. Contends that because this novel is about human redemption through love, Cheever is working "against the grain of most current American fiction." Despite the contrivances and coincidences, Cheever has created mood and character effectively. The result is "one of the most important novels of our time."

79 WILLIAMS, THOMAS. "Cheever's Skill and Imagination Pass Their Most Challenging Test." Chicago Tribune Book World, 13 March, p. 1.
Review of Falconer. Recognizes the presence of a number of symbols but finds that they "resist logical systems of explication." Describes Cheever as a "technically interesting" writer, who has had a "pervasive" influence on other writers.

80 WOLFF, GEOFFREY. "Two Good Fictions." New Times, 1 April, pp. 63-64.
Review of Falconer. Notes that Cheever's most recent works of fiction "have inclined increasingly toward the odd perspectives and dimensions of the dream state" and finds that Falconer fits into this category. Finds this novel "weird," "disturbing," and "tense with a reader's longing for relief and Cheever's refusal to yield it." Concludes that with its controlled plot and a measured, precise diction at times reminiscent of Raymond Chandler, Falconer "is subsersive and menacing art, the most bracing kind."

1978

1 ALLOULA, MALEK. "La memoire du miracle." La Magazine Litteraire (France), April, pp. 35-36.
Review of Falconer. Praises the novel for its originality and finds that it shows "that there is a memory proper to the prison universe, endowed with its own exigencies," especially the subversion of all that denies it.

2 AMORUSO, VITO. "L'America del disinganno" [The America of disappointment]. L'Unita (Italy), 20 September.
Review of Falconer. Sees the novel as representing the turmoil of the soul in the United States, where personal values are lost to collective desires.

3 ANON. Review of Falconer. Bulletin du Libre (France) 385 (May): 887.
Describes Falconer as a "triumph" for Cheever. Praises the powerful, direct style and cinematic techniques.

4   ANON.   "Announcement."   Kirkus Reviews 46 (15 August):   906.
        Review of The Stories of John Cheever.   Considers this
    collection the "rock formation upon which his reputation
    truly rests."   Notes that even though certain of the stories
    are now dated, they still remain "sinfully readable" and
    praises the entire collection as a "mammoth grouping of small,
    polished pleasures."

5   ANON.   "Books."   Playboy 25 (November):   50.
        Review of The Stories of John Cheever.   Sees this collec-
    tion as illustrating "a loss of innocence"; the characters'
    naivete of the earlier Shady Hill pieces is replaced by cyni-
    cism in the subsequent Bullet Park stories.   Yet all of these
    characters are "pulsatingly human."

6   ANON.   "Books."   Vogue 168 (October):   46, 48.
        Review of The Stories of John Cheever.   Sees Cheever's
    great achievement is that "through his eyes, we view reality
    as the complex and magical element it is."   Describes this
    collection as "a map of the author's mind."

7   ANON.   "The Editors' Choice: 1977."   New York Times Book Review,
        1 January, p. 1.
        Notes that Falconer is "a meditation on the abstraction
    Cheever has always called 'home.'"

8   ANON.   "Paperbacks: New and Noteworthy."   New York Times Book
        Review, 29 January, p. 37.
        Notice of paperback publication of Falconer.

9   ANON.   "Paperbacks: New and Noteworthy."   New York Times Book
        Review, 19 February, p. 43.
        Notice of paperback publication of Bullet Park.

10 ANON.   "Some October Titles."   National Review 30 (15 September):
        1155.
        Review of The Stories of John Cheever.   Mentions that this
    collection should be "a real pleasure" to "students of the
    American short story."

11 B., P.   "Fengsel med laste dører" [Prison with locked doors].
        N. Handels og Sjøfarts Tidende (Norway), 23 June.
        Review of Falconer.   Finds the novel so confusing that he
    "cannot undertake a proper guided tour of Falconer prison."

12 BALDICYN, P. V.   "Osobennosti realisticeskoj prozy SSA 60-x
        godov i tvorcestvo Dzona Civera" [The Peculiarities of
        realistic prose in the '60s in the U.S. and the creativity

of John Cheever]. <u>Filologicheskie Nauki</u> (USSR) 1, no. 1: 37–46.

Describes Cheever as one of the principal developers of realistic prose in the 1960s. Discusses his work since the 1930s and notes that in these early years Cheever was not concerned with the proletarian struggle, which dominated much of the American writing of that era. Yet with the publication of <u>The Wapshot Chronicle</u>, Cheever negated bourgeois ideals by revealing the sinister side of capitalism. Finds that Cheever's skeptical view of capitalism is evident through <u>The Wapshot Scandal</u> and even <u>Bullet Park</u>, a dark satire that might have been written by Dostoevski.

13 BANDLER, MICHAEL J.   ". . . And a Conversation with the Story-teller." <u>Chicago Tribune Book World</u>, 22 October, pp. 1, 9.

Interview. Focuses on Cheever's tastes in reading.

14 BANNON, BARBARA. Review of <u>The Stories of John Cheever</u>. <u>Publishers Weekly</u> 214 (14 August): 63.

Describes these stories as "gems, models of limpid prose informed by a clarity of observation and of moral vision that holds vivid and strong." Finds the collection "resonant with feeling and meaning."

15 BECKER, STEPHEN. "Excellence Level in Cheever Short Stories is Astounding." <u>New Orleans Times-Picayune</u>, 9 November, sect. 5, p. 10.

Review of <u>The Stories of John Cheever</u>. Praises these stories for their "consistent and often breathtaking power" and sees Cheever as "one of the two or three most imaginative and acrobatic literary artists now alive." Notes that these stories are more than "slice of life" narrative: "Cheever creates archetypes and essences who work out modern destinies among ancient virtues and vices." Cheever's work deals with human tragedy and buffoonery, loneliness and misunderstanding, "yet he smites us with the variety and sweetness of life, the wonder of being here at all."

16 BOETH, RICHARD. "The Poet of Shady Hill." <u>Newsweek</u> 92 (30 October): 96.

Review of <u>The Stories of John Cheever</u>. The stories here "are capable of reminding us almost too forcefully of how constricted and sealed off" Cheever's world actually is. The pain and snobbery and gin of his characters is "no different from Shylock's or from ours."

17 BRYFONSKI, DEDRIA and MENDELSON, PHYLLIS C., eds. "John Cheever." In <u>Contemporary Literary Criticism</u>. Vol. 8, pp. 136–40. Detroit: Gale Publishing Company.

Reprint of excerpts from: 1977.24; 1977.26; 1977.35; 1977.38; 1977.49; 1977.52; 1977.69; 1977.72.

18 BULTER, WILLEM. "Falconer, de bestseller van John Cheever" [Falconer, John Cheever's bestseller]. Dagblad Tulantia (Netherlands), 24 October.
    Review of Falconer. Attributes its success in America to its documentary-like portrait of prison life. Sees the novel as "thoroughly American" in its presentation of a cross-section of American society.

19 CAVETT, DICK. "The Dick Cavett Show." Public Broadcasting Service. May.
    Interview. Cheever discusses his experience teaching writing and comments on several contemporary writers.

20 CICCO, JUAN. "Una vehemencia perturbadora" [A disturbing force]. La Nacion (Argentina), 28 May.
    Review of Falconer. Describes Cheever as animated by a "mysterious optimism." Finds that he reveals the reality of prison life with "excessive crudity" and notes that he is not a moralist. Instead, Cheever provokes abominable situations and then tries to temper them with notes of humor.

21 CLAPPERTON, JANE. "Cosmo Reads the New Books." Cosmopolitan 185 (December): 16.
    Review of The Stories of John Cheever. Describes this work as a collection of stories "that are consistently, heart-wrenchingly fine."

22 COLUMBO, FURIO. "Quanta morbosita dentro quel carcere" [How Much Morbidity inside Prisons]. Tuttolibri (Italy), 9 September.
    Review of Falconer. Sees this novel as falling within two American traditions: the Protestant, aristocratic ambience of the East, recalling Henry James, and the bad, Catholic conscience of Eugene O'Neill.

23 CORDELLI, FRANCO. "Come Farragut ritrova se stesso" [How Farragut finds himself again]. Paese Sera (Italy), 6 August.
    Review of Falconer. Notes that although Cheever is considered an intellectual in America, in Italy "he is just a commercial writer." Finds that Cheever seems to denounce the permissiveness of society and feels that only in a prison does liberty acquire meaning.

24 CUNNINGHAM, FRANK R. "Cheever's World: Seeing Life Whole." Chronicle of Higher Education Review, 11 December, pp. R6-R7.

1978

       Review of <u>The Stories of John Cheever</u>. Describes these stories as being among the finest written in this country "in any era." Compares his work to that of Hawthorne and James in its "quiet" tone, "disciplined" form and style, and use of the kind, yet judging narrator. Also sees that Cheever's stories "have always been distinguished for their acute psychological vision" and that his realism is tempered by "an acceptance of the tragic as necessary for our psychic health and vigor."

25 CUSHMAN, KEITH. Review of <u>The Stories of John Cheever</u>. <u>Library Journal</u> 103 (15 September): 1766.
       Finds that while some stories among the triumphs here appear to be "self-imitations," and others, such as "The Enormous Radio," are rather "contrived," this collection enables the reader "to truly measure Cheever's substantial achievement."

26 D., F. Review of <u>Falconer</u>. <u>Elle</u> (France), 13 June.
       Notes that while Cheever is unknown in France, this novel is "beautiful" and an "impeccable" example of American writing, with its direct action and rapid, cinematic sequence of scenes.

27 DAHLE, ARVID. "Fengslende fengselroman" [Captivating prison novel]. <u>Adresseavisen</u> (Norway), 13 June.
       Review of <u>Falconer</u>. Cheever's description of prison conditions is so intense that the reader feels like an inmate himself. The prison itself is "a piece of life, a juicy portion of reality," where one meets man in a humiliation that he is occasionally able to rise above. There may well be a trace of black humor, but there is also a relieving light.

28 DAVIS, L. J. "The Books of Christmas: One." <u>Washington Post Book World</u>, 3 December, pp. 1, 16.
       Lists <u>The Stories of John Cheever</u> among the year's major publications.

29 de SANTANA, HUBERT. "In the World of Orchards." <u>Macleans</u>, 4 December, p. 61.
       Biographical essay that includes Cheever's comments on his writing habits and mentions his work on <u>Falconer</u>.

30 _____. "Tripping, Then Stumbling upon the Light Fantastic." <u>Macleans</u>, 4 December, pp. 61–62.
       Review of <u>The Stories of John Cheever</u>. Finds that most of these stories end on an optimistic note that "is rare in modern fiction." Sees Cheever as a subtle moralist who "elevates the commonplace into the universal."

31 DOMMERGUES, PIERRE. "Un Narcisse des tempes modernes" [The
   Narcissus of modern times]. Le Monde (France), 15 September.
      Review of Falconer. Describes the novel as a "beautiful
   book," rich and calm, where irony is constantly present.
   Detects an "aesthetics of discretion" throughout the book,
   which recalls the refined style of the New Yorker.

32 DOTTI, UGO. "Quel tossicomane cerca l'Europa" [The addicted in
   search of Europe]. Messaggero (Italy), 14 October.
      Review of Falconer. Finds that the prison atmosphere
   reveals the American reality of sex, drugs, violence, con-
   sumerism, and prejudice. Sees Cheever as a writer aware of
   his country's crises and thus in search of his European roots.

33 ELLIOTT, GEORGE P. "Fiction and Anti-Fiction." The American
   Scholar 47 (Summer): 398-406.
      In a discussion of contemporary fiction, mentions Falconer
   as Cheever's "strongest book and a defier of labels."

34 EVANS, NANCY. "A Brilliant Peek at All the Rich People."
   Glamour 76 (November): 78.
      Review of The Stories of John Cheever. Finds that the
   characters in these stories have no self-awareness and "love
   their possessions too dearly" to realize "that keeping up
   with the Joneses may be no longer a rare but a losing propo-
   sition." Notes that this collection provides "a beautifully
   crafted glimpse into a life that is becoming extinct."

35 FALDBAKKEN, KNUT. "En hel kultur pa tukthus" [A whole culture
   in prison]. Dagbladet (Norway), 7 June, p. 4.
      Review of Falconer. Finds that this novel, like so many
   other works of modern American literature, has its strength
   in the realistic representation of a milieu. The novel's
   authenticity gives it weight and solidity. However, such
   strength is absent in Cheever's characterization of Farragut,
   perhaps purposely, to depict the modern American stripped of
   his individual qualities, unable to respond humanely in times
   of crisis. Cheever's perceptive and consistently controlled
   inflection in the description of prison life gives the novel
   reverberations far beyond the impact of the ordinary prison
   novel.

36 FRINGELI, DIETER. "Kerker im obszönen Nichts" [Prison in the
   obscene nothingness]. Basler Zeitung (Germany), 18 February.
      Review of Falconer. Attributes the novel's success to its
   concern with social problems. Describes Cheever as an "ex-
   ceptionally nimble and articulate writer" and finds the
   translation "brilliant."

1978

37 FULLER, EDMUND. "A Pride of Short Story Collections." Wall
      Street Jo'rnal, 30 October, p. 24.
          Review of The Stories of John Cheever. Despite a few
      stories that "seem artificial," this collection reveals
      Cheever at his best, as "master chronicler of rueful, anxiety-
      ridden middle-class" suburbanites.

38 GARDNER, JOHN. "A Cheever Milestone: 61 Elegantly Crafted
      Stories." Chicago Tribune Book World, 22 October, p. 1.
          Review of The Stories of John Cheever. Includes Cheever
      among the "major figures in contemporary American letters"
      and describes these stories as "realistic in the best sense
      of the word." While some pieces in this collection are
      clearly products of a certain era, they resist being "dated"
      because of Cheever's "perfected craftsmanship."

39 _____. "Moral Fiction." Saturday Review 5 (1 April): pp. 29-30,
      32-33.
          Considers Bullet Park and Falconer. Finds that "Cheever's
      writing has importance" and that he balances "his optimistic
      Christian vision with the necessary measure of irony."
      Adapted from 1978.40.

40 _____. On Moral Fiction. New York: Basic Books, pp. 97-98.

41 GRAY, PAUL. "Inescapable Conclusions." Time 112 (16 October):
      122, 125.
          Review of The Stories of John Cheever. Finds that these
      stories are "almost better than people remember" and that now
      the idea of a typical Cheever story seems "further from the
      more complex and entertaining truth." Compares the best of
      these stories to fulcrums, in that "they translate consider-
      able social weight into emotional power." Review followed by
      brief profile and interview, in which Cheever comments on his
      life and his current writing.

42 GRIESER, DIETMAR. "Ausgesperrt--weil ich Mensch bin" [Shut out--
      because I am human]. Welt am Sonntag (Germany), 16 April.
          Review of Falconer. Contends that Falconer's American
      success is not explicable, except by the considerable role
      that homosexuality plays in American literary taste.

43 GRILLANDI, TELESIO. "Prigioniero della droga" [The prisoner of
      drugs]. Giornale di Bergamo (Italy), 6 June.
          Review of Falconer. Praises Cheever's sense of detail and
      his attention to the smallest sensations. Finds that although
      Farragut's life evolves in a prison, it still reveals much
      about American society.

44 HABERMAN, CLYDE and KREBS, ALBIN. "A Fan Fans Tiant." New York
    Times, 29 November, p. C-18.
        Notes that while speaking before a Boston literary society
    yesterday, Cheever groused "mightily about the recent defec-
    tion of Luis Tiant, the pitcher, from the Red Sox to the
    Yankees." Cheever added: "All literary men are Red Sox
    fans. . . . To be a Yankee fan in literary society is to
    endanger your life."

45 HERSEY, JOHN. "John Cheever, Boy and Man." New York Times Book
    Review, 26 March, pp. 3, 31-34.
        Reprints a major part of 1977.40.

46 IRVING, JOHN. "Facts of Living." Saturday Review 5
    (30 September): 44-46.
        Review of The Stories of John Cheever. Surveys a number
    of these stories and finds that their variety and the "con-
    stancy of Cheever's careful voice give this collection the
    breadth and wholeness of the biggest of novels." Admires the
    success with which these pieces affirm humanity and concludes
    that Cheever is our best living storyteller.

47 JENSSON, ARNFINN. "Falconer: En roman om frihet" [Falconer:
    A novel about freedom]. Lofotposten (Norway), 31 July.
        Review of Falconer. Finds that Cheever is able to evoke
    sentiments among his readers "without particularly stressing
    anything." Notes that the novel captivates one, even though
    it is not composed "like a thriller."

48 KAPP, ISA. "The Cheerless World of John Cheever." The New
    Leader 61 (11 September): 16-17.
        Review of The Stories of John Cheever. Argues that despite
    the parallels suggested by a number of critics between Chekhov
    and Cheever, Chekhov sympathized with his characters, whereas
    "Cheever's sympathies spring unaccountably back to the observer,
    as if he were personally affronted, violated in his finer sen-
    sibilities by the shabby tales he relates." In most of
    Cheever's stories, his outlook is grim, and often he "juxta-
    poses the pleasing prospect of nature and the disagreeable
    one of men and women, and lurches so readily from cynicism
    to exaltation." Thus it is in a novel like Falconer, where
    Cheever is able to confront the "blackness in himself," that
    his fiction becomes "strong and plausible."

49 KIRSCH, ROBERT. "Master Storytelling in the Fiction of Cheever
    and Shaw." Los Angeles Times Book Review, 26 November,
    pp. 1, 37.

1978

Review of <u>The Stories of John Cheever</u>. Finds these "engrossing" stories "better than remembered," and the collection "is something more than the sum of its parts." At the center of the collection "is the sense of a master storyteller intent on delivering that compressed narrative, . . . the ironic or emotive mood, the hint of values fragmenting which brings us into the center of Cheever's time and people." The book conveys an understanding of "the way we lived and dreamed then and now."

50 KREBS, ALBIN. "Notes on People." <u>New York Times</u>, 14 February, p. 32.
    Notes that Cheever will be among the "luminaries from the literary world" who will pay tribute to Saul Bellow on February 23, when Bellow will receive the 1978 Gold Medal of Honor from the National Arts Club in Manhattan.

51 L., J. D. "Una ancha zona de pesar" [A wide zone of importance]. <u>Revista Confirando</u> (Argentina), 29 June, p. 36.
    Review of <u>Falconer</u>. Finds that Cheever evokes a bitter and dissolute world in this novel. His use of the prison as a microcosm is reminiscent of similar effects created in <u>Robinson Crusoe</u> and <u>Moby Dick</u>, though Cheever's mood is perturbing, uncomfortable, and fascinating.

52 La POLLA, FRANCO. "Dietro la rispettabilita c'e corruzione e nevrosi" [Behind respectability there is corruption and neurosis]. <u>Il Resto Del Carlino</u> (Italy), 12 August.
    Review of <u>Falconer</u>. Contends that Cheever uses Farragut to depict the corruption and neurosis that exists behind the facade of the bourgeois American family.

53 LEEDOM-ACKERMAN, JOANNE. "Cheever's Stories Leap the Suburban Fence." <u>Christian Science Monitor</u>, 23 October, p. B-18.
    Review of <u>The Stories of John Cheever</u>. Finds that while the prose is generally "clear and precise," the skill exhibited in the stories is uneven: "the lapses appear to coincide not so much with the author's inexperience as with his periodic inability to match his ambition to his characters." Finds that this collection, depicting weak women and ambitious, if occasionally fumbling men, as a "whole is better than its finely crafted parts."

54 LEONARD, JOHN. "Books of the Times." <u>New York Times</u>, 7 November, p. 43.
    Review of <u>The Stories of John Cheever</u>. Finds that Cheever's chronicle of "the decline of <u>his</u> social class . . . is as deft and luminous as the accounts of Waugh and Proust"; yet Cheever

is more charitable than both of these writers combined. Contends that the publication of this collection is "a grand occasion in English literature."

55 LOCKE, RICHARD. "Visions of Order and Domestic Disarray." New York Times Book Review, 3 December, pp. 3, 78.
    Review of The Stories of John Cheever. Sees Cheever neither as a satirist nor as a celebrant of the suburbs, but as a "tender" writer "concerned with evoking his characters' nostalgia." Compares these stories to Schubert's sonatas, in that both are repetitious and sentimental yet "beautiful," and describes Cheever's gift as "the power to present a sensuous . . . detail that effortlessly carries intense emotional and symbolic force." Comments also on the relationships between Cheever's novels and stories and between Cheever and Hawthorne, Updike, and Bellow.

56 LUNDKVIST, ARTUR. "En effektiv fängelsefantasi" [An effective prison fantasy]. Arbetet (Sweden), 11 November.
    Review of Falconer. Finds the novel balanced remarkably between the most tangible naturalism and a kind of hope struggling toward the light. It is a liberation for Farragut to force his way down to the rocky base of existence, tossing aside all pretense and deception, at last to experience himself and others entirely as they are. This book is "tremendously effective in its sharp-etched, heavily charged presentation."

57 McPHERSON, WILLIAM. "The Books of Christmas: 2." Washington Post Book World, 10 December, pp. 1, 8.
    Includes The Stories of John Cheever among the year's best books and notes that Cheever's fictive world "is so precisely, glowingly and tellingly rendered that whatever limitations that world may have . . . are transcended by the storyteller's art."

58 _____. "Cheever By the Dozen." Washington Post Book World, 22 October, pp. 1, 6.
    Review of The Stories of John Cheever. Finds Cheever's "compellingly readable" stories to be "simply, the best." Compares Cheever to Chekhov, since both write about "a fragile society in which the glue is crumbling and turning to powder, but the weight of time and memory keeps the old, still valuable pieces tenuously in place: until they suffer some rude shock . . . and the forms fail to hold."

59 MITGANG, HERBERT. "Bellow Gets Arts Medal of Honor." New York Times, 24 February, p. C-28.

1978

>   Notes that Malamud and Cheever were the principal speakers
> on the program, and that Cheever referred to Bellow as a "mas-
> ter of his time."

60 MOHN, BENT. "Fald og frelse" [Fall and redemption]. <u>Politiken</u>
   (Denmark), 11 October.
>   Review of <u>Falconer</u>. Finds that in contrast to the loosely
> organized Wapshot novels, <u>Falconer</u> is tightly "riveted to-
> gether, with a steadily rising curve of suspense."

61 NICOL, CHARLES. "The Truth, The Impartial Truth." <u>Harper's</u>
   257 (October): 93-95.
>   Review of <u>The Stories of John Cheever</u>. Finds that these
> stories usually "set up extreme tensions between what should
> be believed and what must be seen." Attributes this consis-
> tency to the fact that these stories date from the mid-1940s,
> when Cheever had achieved "a mature vision if not a fully
> mature style."

62 PIETRAVALLE, NICOLETTA. "Il prigioniero di Falconer" [The
   prisoner of Falconer]. <u>Il Tempo</u> (Italy), 13 October.
>   Review of <u>Falconer</u>. Contends that the importance of this
> novel does not lie in Farragut's story but in Cheever's detail-
> ing precisely what enables the prisoners to survive. His de-
> piction of the emotional and physical needs of the prisoners
> is the major source of suspense here.

63 REIBSTEIN, JOAN NATALIE. "John Cheever." In <u>Britannica Book
   of the Year: 1978</u>, p. 85. Chicago: Encyclopedia Britannica.
>   Finds that the publication of <u>Falconer</u> "solidified the
> author's reputation as a major American novelist as well as
> one of the foremost contemporary short-story writers." In-
> cludes brief biography.

64 RIVIERE, FRANCOIS. Review of <u>Falconer</u>. <u>Les Nouvelles
   Litteraires</u> (France), 16 June.
>   Describes this novel as an "admirable fable composed with
> an uncommon spirit," which naturally takes its place beside
> the strongest works of Salinger, Roth, and Bellow.

65 SCHICKEL, RICHARD. "The Cheever Chronicle." <u>Horizon</u> 21
   (September): 28-33.
>   Discusses Cheever's career and notes that his art has been
> sustained throughout the years by the perception "that the
> world is infinitely more variable, far richer in wonders . . .
> than we are brought up to believe it is" and by a tension that
> derives from a balance of his sense of life's tragedy with an
> "equally strong appreciation of our sheer craziness."

Comments on Cheever's use of the balance of light and dark
and notes that in Falconer "Cheever permitted himself an un-
characteristic note of triumph." Describes Cheever as a
visionary who is also a moralist and finds that even as he
grows older, he "cannot bring himself to embrace despair
totally."

66 SCHLOZ, GÜNTHER. "Die Flucht vor Ausflüchten" [The escape from
evasion]. Deutsche Zeitung, 3 March.
Review of Falconer. Describes this novel as "a book of
hope," in which Cheever does not moralize but "trusts in the
power of poetry" to make plausible Farragut's escape. Even
the unsatisfactory German translation cannot spoil the quality
of this novel.

67 SHAW, IRWIN. "Cheever Country." Bookviews 2 (October): 56-57.
Review of The Stories of John Cheever. Describes Cheever
as "a judge of stern moral standards." Finds that these stories are crafted "in an elegant, sonorous, guileful prose"
and "with a high decorum that he has raised to one of the
prime virtues of his art."

68 SHAW, ROBERT B. "The World in A Very Small Space." Nation 227
(23 December): 705-7.
Review of The Stories of John Cheever. Finds the collection "prodigious, and deeply engaging," but suspects that the
attention Cheever has received is more a by-product of his
four novels than of his short fiction. Notes that throughout
this collection, it is striking how frequently Cheever's characters "take refuge in memory from the depredations of the
present." Also, since Cheever is more an "explorer of the
further reaches of our moral awareness" than a "promoter of
gentility," his finer stories tend to assume mythic dimensions.

69 SHENKER, ISRAEL. "Solzhenitsyn, in Harvard Speech, Terms West
Weak and Cowardly." New York Times, 9 June, p. 8.
Notes that at the June 8th Harvard commencement, Cheever
received an honorary degree.

70 S[INCLAIR], D[OROTHY]. Review of The Stories of John Cheever.
West Coast Review of Books 4 (November): 39-40.
Suggests that this collection represents Cheever's quest
"into the nature of ourselves within our environments." Surveys a number of these stories, finds that "O City of Broken
Dreams" is among the best, and praises Cheever's ability to
stimulate the reader throughout, both emotionally and
intellectually.

1978

71 TAANING, TAGE. "Amerikansk mestervaerk" [American masterwork].
    Berlingske Tidende (Denmark), 5 October.
         Review of Falconer. Finds the "poetic realism" of this
    novel comparable to that of The Great Gatsby. Praises
    Cheever's satiric, "baroque imagination."

72 TAVERNIER-COURBIN, JACQUELINE, and COLLINS, R. G. "An Interview
    with John Cheever." THALIA: Studies in Literary Humor 1
    (Spring): 3-9.
         Interview. Cheever comments on humor in literature and its
    relation to style. Also gives his opinion on the fiction of
    Gass, Barth, Barthelme, and Coover and notes that it is "un-
    fortunate that we should try classifying" authors such as
    Hemingway, Faulkner, and Fitzgerald as belonging to a certain
    generation or period. Refuses to assess his own work and
    hopes his future writing will be "an improvement over what
    I've done."

73 TOWERS, ROBERT. "Light Touch." New York Review of Books,
    9 November, pp. 3-4.
         Review of The Stories of John Cheever. Decribes Cheever
    as "an old-fashioned lyric poet," who, like Lawrence and
    Faulkner, is able to use vivid imagery "as an essential ele-
    ment in the lives and moods of his characters." However, un-
    like Faulkner, Cheever is unable to depict characters con-
    vincingly who are not of the upper-middle class and instead
    "settles for faintly embarrassing stereotypes." Still, the
    many successes collected in this volume allow the few trivial
    or flawed stories to "recede to their proper place."

74 TRIMMER, JOSEPH F., ed. The National Book Awards for Fiction:
    An Index to the First Twenty-Five Years. Boston: G. K.
    Hall, pp. 109-15, passim.
         Notes that Cheever won the National Book Award for The
    Wapshot Chronicle in 1958 and traces the success of Cheever's
    subsequent books and his own work as a judge for the 1964 and
    1971 awards.

75 TYLER, ANNE. "Books Considered." New Republic 179
    (4 November): 45-47.
         Review of The Stories of John Cheever. Finds that reading
    the entire "dazzling" collection has the effect of reading a
    novel. Distinguishes between two types of stories present
    here: those "written from the outside," which take a cool or
    ironic tone, and those "written from the inside," where even
    bleak events are transformed by the "sunny vision of the nar-
    rator." The former type leaves the reader feeling embittered,
    while the latter type is often poignant, and even borders on
    the mythic.

76 _____. "The Books of Christmas: One." <u>Washington Post Book World</u>, 3 December, pp. 1, 14.
    Lists <u>The Stories of John Cheever</u> among her "favorite books of 1978" and praises it for the "dense, full world it unfolds before us."

77 VARNER, JAN. "Frodig humor og brutal realisme" [Exuberant humor and harsh reality]. <u>Morgenbladet</u> (Norway), 8 August.
    Review of <u>Falconer</u>. Detects, in the portrayal of Farragut and the other inmates, elements of burlesque and exuberant humor, like a sparkling Henry Miller at his best. Cheever's style is difficult to describe but seems vivid, poignant, and harshly realistic. In addition, his writing has a peculiar dreamlike quality to it. This novel is "the work of a poet."

78 WILLIAMS, JOY. "Meaningful Fiction . . . John Cheever's Stories are Memorable." <u>Esquire</u> 90 (21 November): 35-36.
    Review of <u>The Stories of John Cheever</u>. Praises Cheever for celebrating "our bewildering lives" in these resonant, evocative stories. Though "Cheever writes <u>sad</u> stories," he renders a mundane world "beautiful, comical, and true" through his artistry.

79 WOLFE, GEOFFREY. "Cheever's Chain of Being." <u>New Times</u>, 27 November, pp. 84, 86.
    Review of <u>The Stories of John Cheever</u>. Considers these stories to be "the most consistently scrupulous body of prose any living American has made." Praises Cheever's "accuracy of sentiment and moral judgment" and notes that often throughout his canon runs "the litany of despair," notably in stories such as "The Enormous Radio." Finds that Cheever writes "of darkness looking for light."

80 ZANDELIN, PIA. "Pia Zandelin möter John Cheever" [Pia Zandelin meets John Cheever]. <u>Expressen</u> (Sweden), 31 October.
    Profile-interview. Cheever speaks of his years publishing in the <u>New Yorker</u> and of his friendship with Dorothy Parker. Zandelin sees in <u>Falconer</u> a likeness of Vonnegut's <u>Slaughterhouse Five</u> and considers Cheever's "thirst for life" similar to that expressed by Emily Dickinson.

1979

1 ALLEN, HENRY. "John Cheever: Capturing the Splendors of Suburbia." <u>Washington Post</u>, 8 October, pp. B-1, 13.
    Interview. Cheever discusses the forthcoming Public Broadcasting Service broadcast of three of his stories and his "delight in the whole project." Also comments on the theme

of nostalgia in his work, his problems with alcohol, and his
life in New England.

2 AMIEL, BARBARA. "Best, Worst and Others of 1978." <u>Macleans</u>,
8 January, p. 46.
Lists <u>The Stories of John Cheever</u> among the nine best
books of the year.

3 ANON. Review of <u>The Stories of John Cheever</u>. <u>Choice</u> 15
(February): 1662.
Finds that Cheever "has come a long way in recent years
from cult taste to established master of the short story form."
Describes this publication as "a major publishing event."

4 ANON. "Academy-Institute to Elect Head." <u>New York Times</u>,
23 January, p. C-20.
Notes that Cheever is secretary of the American Academy and
Institute of Arts and Letters.

5 ANON. "NBCC Names 1978 Annual Award Winners." <u>Publishers Weekly</u>
215 (22 January): 282.
Reports that <u>The Stories of John Cheever</u> was chosen as the
best fiction work of 1978 by the National Book Critics Circle.

6 ANON. "The Post Recommends." <u>Saturday Evening Post</u> 251
(March): 91.
Review of <u>The Stories of John Cheever</u>. Describes these
stories as "different yet all similar" in that most of them
"peel away the outer skin of well-heeled suburbia and dig
into the raw flesh of its inhabitants." Finds that these
pieces "are well-written, well-plotted, and heavy with under-
lying meaning."

7 ANON. "Sketches of Winners of Pulitzer Prizes in Journalism,
the Arts and Letters." <u>New York Times</u>, 17 April, p. B-8.
Notes that Cheever is known for his "pellucid prose style."
Includes a brief biographical note.

8 BAILEY, PAUL. "Tales of suburbia." <u>Observer</u> (London), 10 June,
p. 37.
Review of <u>The Stories of John Cheever</u>. Considers this
collection to contain "some of the best short fiction written
on either side of the Atlantic since the war." Finds that
among the significant recurrent images in Cheever's stories
are light and water: "People are consoled by the first and
cleansed by the latter." Contends that Cheever is better
writing short fiction than novels, because in the former,
character need only be "hinted at," and Cheever is "wonderful

when he's hinting, but his explanations . . . aren't always acceptable." Concludes that Cheever's lyrical effects are more successful when kept "in a minor key."

9 BARBATO, JOSEPH. "The Short Story: Its Fortunes and Follies." Chicago Tribune Book World, 29 July, pp. 1, 3.
    Surveys the status of the short story form in America today. Includes comments by Cheever on the short fiction writer's need for "a responsive and mature audience."

10 BELL, PEARL K. "Literary Waifs." Commentary 67 (February): 67-71.
    Sees the "abiding theme" of The Stories of John Cheever as disappointment "with the way life has, alas, turned out." Notes that while his strength lies in his ability to grasp "social detail," the America of his fiction "seems airless and timeless" because it is devoid of any allusions to contemporary history or politics.

11 BRADBURY, MALCOLM. "Better Times." New Statesman 97 (29 June): 956-57.
    Review of The Stories of John Cheever. Finds that in this collection Cheever established and maintained his themes early, "so that later pieces seem like mature reflections on earlier themes and characters." Places Cheever between Fitzgerald and Updike "in an intermediate generation, an intermediate form" and notes that Cheever is "a storyteller of the wealthy," who writes "the swansong of an American aristocracy in a lowered world." Yet, praises his control and a management of tone that seems to give his stories "several existences."

11a BRAUDY, LEO. "Realists, Naturalists, and Novelists of Manners." In Harvard Guide to Contemporary American Writing. Edited by Daniel Hoffman, pp. 143-44, 146, 148. Cambridge, Ma.: Harvard University Press, Belknap Press.
    Finds that Cheever's principal concern is with "understanding the compromises and the repressions of . . . the upwardly dispossessed." Notes that Cheever's "epiphany-seeking vision" is most effective in his short fiction.

12 BRESLIN, JOHN B. "John Cheever in the Critics' Circle." America 140 (17 February): 115-16.
    Review of The Stories of John Cheever. Finds the collection "filled with nostalgia" and terms Cheever "our best prose stylist with a fine ear for the verbal foibles that make his generation's talk and that of their elders and children unmistakable." Mentions that the collection won the National

1979

Book Critics Circle Award and quotes from Cheever's acceptance speech.

13 COATES, DENNIS. "John Cheever: A Checklist, 1930-1978." <u>Bulletin of Bibliography</u> 36 (January): 1-13, 49.
    Provides primary and secondary bibliographies of Cheever's work. Lists many of the American and some of the English reviews through <u>Falconer</u>.

14 CRAIG, PATRICIA. Review of <u>The Stories of John Cheever</u>. <u>Books and Bookmen</u> 24 (August): 62-63.
    Finds that Cheever scrutinizes the American middle class "with detachment, tempered by irony." Observes that "moral and social implications" increase in complexity, throughout this collection and reach "a high-water-mark" in "The World of Apples." Notes also that Cheever's "deeply ironic vision has saved him from the pressure of nostalgia, though he may arouse this emotion in an impressionable reader."

15 FREEMONT-SMITH, ELIOT. "25 for '78." <u>Village Voice</u> 24 (1 January): 72.
    Lists <u>The Stories of John Cheever</u> among the twenty-five nominees for the National Book Critics Circle Award and notes that the most famous of Cheever's stories are about "WASPs in trouble; they sing and hurt, and get hurt, and decline to fade away."

16 GRIFFIN, BRYAN F. "Literary Vogues: Getting Cheever while he's hot." <u>Harper's</u> 258 (June): 90-93.
    Surveys the enthusiastic critical reception Cheever has received since <u>Falconer</u>, which has endowed his canon with "retroactive profundity." Contends that <u>Falconer</u> is merely "a shallow puddle of implausibility" that wants to be taken seriously. Laments the excessive praise of such a "minor" artist: "there was definitely a place for John Cheever. They should have left him there."

17 GUERESCHI, EDWARD. Review of <u>The Stories of John Cheever</u>. <u>Best Sellers</u> 38 (February): 337-38.
    Calls Cheever "our greatest lyrical writer of that vanishing species, the upper middle-class." Finds that Cheever is able to "capture the happy rhythm of family life" and "evoke sensory texture of time and place with disarming brilliance." But he is "most eloquent" when describing his characters' journeys to self-exploration in stories such as "The Swimmer."

18 HILL, DOUG. "The Bite of the Termite." <u>Books in Canada</u> 8 (February): 19-20.

Review of The Stories of John Cheever. Sees a resemblance in "the attitudes and talents" of F. Scott Fitzgerald to those of Cheever. Compares the small effects of Cheever's "romantic irony" over his long career to those of a termite. Praises Cheever's "sure" style, "dazzling" assurance, and facility to generate meaning from the "sound and rhythm and metaphor" of language.

19 HOWARD, JANE. "Superb." Mademoiselle 85 (January): 44.
Review of The Stories of John Cheever. Finds that the searches made by Cheever's characters "have a poignant valor about them."

20 HUNT, GEORGE. "Beyond the Cheeveresque: A Style Both Lyrical and Idiosyncratic." Commonweal 106 (19 January): 20-22.
Review of The Stories of John Cheever. Maintains that despite the conventional critical response to Cheever, which labels him a "sociologist in disguise," Cheever is an artist concerned with "the mystery of the human and its corollary, the mystery of language." Cheever's thematic concerns are similar to those of Bellow and Updike, and while all three are versatile stylists, "Cheever's prose almost demands that it be read aloud." When lyrical, Cheever's style is reminiscent of the later poetry of Yeats; when idiosyncratic, it recalls the later Auden. In addition, Cheever's "comic technique" is like Auden's, in that it continually shifts "stylistic gears from fantasy to realism." The fact that Cheever's humor is "consistently hilarious" and has the "qualities of a yarn," furthermore, places him in the American tradition of Mark Twain, Ring Lardner, and Damon Runyon. Concludes that in his "sympathy with his characters' fallen state," Cheever "is deeply Christian in sensibility."

21 KAHN, E. J., JR. About the "New Yorker" and Me. New York: G. P. Putnam's Sons, pp. 160-61, 244-45, passim.
Memoir spanning 1977. Kahn recounts his experiences at the New Yorker with Cheever.

22 KAKUTANI, MICHIKO. "In a Cheever-Like Setting, John Cheever Gets MacDowell Medal." New York Times, 11 September, p. C-7.
Reports that Cheever is the twentieth recipient of the annual Edward MacDowell Medal. Discusses Cheever's work and quotes from Elizabeth Hardwick's speech in which she traced "the maturation of Mr. Cheever's vision."

23 KENNEDY, EUGENE. Review of The Stories of John Cheever. The Critic 37 (February): 4, 8.

1979

Praises Cheever not only for his craftmanship, but also
because he has been providing his readers, "quite uncon-
sciously, with a theology of our age." Finds that Cheever
is more "an artist of moral sensitivity" than a "flamboyant
moralist" and that his Christian vision of contemporary life
is essentially tragic.

24 KIHSS, PETER. "Shepard Takes Pulitzer for Drama, Baker of <u>Times</u>
Wins for Comment." <u>New York Times</u>, 17 April, p. 1.
Reports that Cheever won the Pulitzer Prize for <u>The Stories
of John Cheever</u>.

25 KING, FRANCIS. "Making it New." <u>Spectator</u> 242 (23 June):
29-30.
Review of <u>The Stories of John Cheever</u>. Notes that while
Cheever's "vision of life as joyous, exciting and beautiful"
has led many to compare him with Chekhov and Lawrence, "it is
with Katherine Mansfield that he has the closest affinity."
Sees this similarity borne out even in both writers' capacity
for "feline scratchiness" and in their "deplorable lapses
into archness and sentimentality." Finds "The Swimmer" to be
the best story of the collection and "one of the dozen best
short-stories ever written" and sees Cheever and James Purdy
as America's "greatest" contemporary writers.

26 KORNBLUTH, JESSE. "The Cheever Chronicle." <u>New York Times
Magazine</u>, 21 October, pp. 26-29, 102-05.
Anecdotal account of Cheever's present life and writing at
Ossining, New York. Suggests, despite Cheever's objection,
that his fiction "is mostly opaque autobiography" and then
attempts to draw parallels between his writings and his life.
Also discusses Cheever's interest in religion, which "he has
personalized as the pursuit of radiance."

27 MASON, KENNETH C. "Bookmarks." <u>Prairie Schooner</u> 53 (Spring):
92.
Review of <u>The Stories of John Cheever</u>. Sees Cheever as an
affirmative realist who avoids sentimentality. Finds "the
great breadth of Cheever's imaginative vision" in these stories "most impressive" and maintains that each story is
Cheever's "fresh attempt to save a part of our world from
time." At least six of these stories are "fit to stand"
with the short fiction of Hawthorne, Hemingway, and Singer.

28 MEYER, ARLIN G. "A Garden of Love After Eden." <u>The Cresset</u> 42
(June): 22-28.
Review of <u>The Stories of John Cheever</u>. Describes this
collection as "a garden of love and erotic horseplay [and]

also a garden of delight and color." Discusses a number of
the stories in detail and traces the dominant themes that
recur in Cheever's fiction, noting that he is concerned with
family, home, and place. Suspects that his use of "images of
light and dream are ultimately clues to transcendence in
Cheever's fiction."

29 MITGANG, HERBERT. "Behind the Bestsellers: John Cheever."
   New York Times Book Review, 28 January, p. 36.
      Interview. Cheever describes how his stories originate
   and how he differs from John Updike. Explains also that he
   avoids "looking for a story" in contemporary news but sees
   his major themes as "love and death."

30 _____. "National Book Critics Prize To Stories of John Cheever."
   New York Times, 16 January, p. 9.
      Notes that Cheever won the 1978 National Book Critics
   Circle award in fiction on a second ballot.

31 MULLINS, JOHN J. "Cheever Writes on Matters of Urgency." New
   Orleans Times-Picayune, 22 February, sect. 4, p. 6.
      Interview. Cheever comments on his work and notes that he
   is "not inclined to think of myself as being remembered for
   anything." Finds that much literature "that is splendid is
   splendid only for a very brief period of time."

32 O'CONNOR, JOHN J. "TV: A Series of Stories by John Cheever
   Begins." New York Times, 24 October, p. C-28.
      Notes that the Public Broadcasting Service telecast of
   three of Cheever's stories will begin tonight. Finds that
   the first of these stories, "The Sorrows of Gin," "resists
   electronic assimilation. . . . The Cheever subtlety is lost
   in a torrent of obvious references." The result is that the
   first of this series "remains curiously lifeless."

33 _____. "TV: Cheever's 'O Youth and Beauty!' on WNET." New
   York Times, 31 October, p. C-31.
      Describes this Public Broadcasting Service broadcast as a
   "sensible adaptation." Finds that "the smooth agony of
   Mr. Cheever's story is caught almost painfully in this television production."

34 _____. "TV: Cheever Puts Terror on the 5:48." New York Times,
   7 November, p. C-32.
      Notes that despite the dramatic license that is "heavily
   invoked" in the adaptation of "The Five Forty-Eight," "the
   overall tone of the piece remains faithful to Mr. Cheever."
   Finds that this series of three stories has demonstrated

1979

"that American literature can serve as an important source of dramatic material."

35 OLSON, CLARENCE E. "If It Hadn't Been For Cheever." St. Louis Post-Dispatch, 21 January, p. 4-F.
    Surveys the 1978 contenders for the National Book Critics Circle awards and argues that John Irving's The World According to Garp would have won the fiction award had Cheever's collection of stories not been published in 1978. While praising Cheever's book as "the most stunning collection of short stories to be published in several decades," the author laments the "unfairness" of pitting Cheever against Irving, "the most promising young novelist of the decade."

36 RICKENBACKER, WILLIAM F. "Visions of Grace." National Review 31 (13 April): 491-93.
    Review of The Stories of John Cheever. Finds that Cheever's vision is mysterious in the liturgical sense, with the "cartographers of Cheever country" being Matthew, Mark, Luke, and John. Notes that Cheever uses random violence in his fiction to compel his readers "to deal with the Glad Tidings as if they were headlines in today's newspaper."

37 SAVAGE, J. W. "John Cheever: the Long and the Short and the Tall." Chicago Tribune Magazine, 22 April, pp. 30-1, 33, 35.
    Profile. Speculates on Cheever's chance to receive the Nobel Prize in 1979 and notes that there was similar speculation in 1976 and 1977. Discusses Cheever's life and career and includes Cheever's comments on literature.

38 _____. "The Works of John Cheever." Chicago Tribune Magazine, 22 April, p. 35.
    Surveys Cheever's work and notes that Cheever "exploits the foibles, examines the results, and at times satirizes the cadence to which we march."

39 SMILGIS, MARTHA. "The Dark Moments of His Life Rival--and Perhaps Inspire--John Cheever's Stories." People 11 (23 April): 78-80, 83.
    Biographical profile which includes Cheever's comments on his life and work. He mentions his recently completed Public Broadcasting Service television script, "The Shady Hill Kidnapping," and his work in progress, a "long book" that he will not elaborate on.

40 SMITH, CECIL. "KCET: 3 Nights of Cheever." Los Angeles Times, 24 October, Part IV, p. 19.

Discusses the Public Broadcasting Service broadcast of
Cheever's three stories. Focuses on Wendy Wasserstein's
adaptation of "The Sorrows of Gin." Smith is "delighted"
that she "did not hold to the Cheever line but widened and
deepened the story."

40a SWICK, MARLY A. "Romantic Ministers and Phallic Knights: A
Study of A Month of Sundays, Lancelot, and Falconer." Ph.D.
dissertation, American University, 42 pp.
Finds that these novels share the theme of "the desaciliza-
tion of the universe." Updike, Percy and Cheever depict a
culture where "the loss of faith is . . . accompanied by the
loss of sexual virility and a fear of impotence."

41 TYLER, RALPH. "How a Trio of Cheever Stories made it to TV."
New York Times, 14 October, pp. B-1, 33.
Discusses the Public Broadcasting Service adaptations of
Cheever's stories and the playwrights who wrote the teleplays.
Notes that "Cheever's somewhat spare elegance and ability to
make what he leaves out as important as what he puts in are
not so easy to dramatize."

42 UNGER, ARTHUR. "John Cheever Buffs Should Be Relieved."
Christian Science Monitor, 22 October, p. 19.
Describes the three stories adapted for Public Broadcasting
Service broadcast as "studies in the varieties of isolation."
Previews each adaptation and considers the whole enterprise
"a major step forward in PBS's ongoing attempt to bring Amer-
ican literature to American television."

43 _____. "John Cheever's Long View." Christian Science Monitor,
24 October, pp. 17-18.
Interview. Cheever discusses the adaptations of his three
stories for the Public Broadcasting Service and his perception
of his audience. Comments on the publication of his work in
communist countries, noting that only in Bulgaria has Falconer
been published in translation. Notes that despite his writing
an original one-hour drama for the Public Broadcasting Service,
"The Shady Hill Kidnapping," he would not like to continue
writing for television permanently.

44 WALDELAND, LYNNE. John Cheever. Boston: Twayne Publishers.
Surveys Cheever's literary career through Falconer. Sees
Cheever as having "Emerson's faith in the potential for great-
ness of human beings and Thoreau's careful eye and love for
the beauty of the natural world." He also has a "Hawthornian
awareness" of psychology and a "Jamesian understanding" of

1979

mores and motives. Finds Cheever's style, with its "beauty
and consistency," to be the "most remarkable aspect" of his
career. Includes chronology and selected primary and secondary bibliographies.

45 WIDEBRANT, MATS. "En ensamhet som förändrar allt" [A loneliness
that changes all]. Götesborgs-Posten (Sweden), 22 January.
Review of Falconer. Describes the novel as "no easy book."
Finds that Falconer is filled with feelings that always lie
beneath the surface and that demand concentration and reflection to discern. At the same time these feelings give life
and meaning to the external action. Considers the prison itself as an evil that must and can be defeated, because for
Cheever the "day of miracles is not yet past."

46 YARDLEY, JONATHAN. "The State of American Fiction." Commonweal
106 (11 May): 265-66.
Finds that contemporary American fiction is "healthy,
lively and consequential" and includes The Stories of John
Cheever among the five recent "books of lasting value and
importance."

Index